Interactional Psychotherapy

**Stages and Strategies
in Behavioral Change**

Interactional Psychotherapy

Stages and Strategies
in Behavioral Change

Sheldon Cashdan, Ph.D.

University of Massachusetts
Amherst, Massachusetts

GRUNE & STRATTON
A subsidiary of Harcourt Brace Jovanovich, Publishers
New York and London

Library of Congress Cataloging in Publication Data

Cashdan, Sheldon.
    Interactional psychotherapy.

    Bibliography: p.
    1. Psychotherapy. I. Title. [DNLM: 1. Psycho-
therapy. WM 420 C338i 1973]
RC480.C33   616.8'914   73-5764
ISBN 0-8089-0809-X

Grune & Stratton, Inc.
111 Fifth Avenue
New York, New York 10003

Library of Congress Catalog Card Number 73-5764
International Standard Book Number 0-8089-0809-X

Printed in the United States of America

For David and Jessica

Contents

	Preface	xi
1	The Process of Psychotherapy	1
2	The Practice of Psychotherapy	13
3	Theory of Interactional Change	42
4	Interactional Individual Therapy	62
5	Interactional Group Therapy	102
	Bibliography	139
	Index	145

Preface

The psychotherapist is a professional who has to deal with difficult subject matter. Human behavior is everchanging, not easily amenable to quantification, and presents itself in irrational as well as rational ways. Considering our preference for consistency and rationality, human beings with psychological troubles are somewhat inconsiderate of psychotherapists—especially those who are still apprentices.

To compound this difficulty, the therapist must master a "technique" in order to solve or ameliorate the problems which confront him. The technique consists, in part, of knowing *how* as well as *when* to say something therapeutic. Conducting therapy, however, involves more than learning techniques and memorizing a cookbook of statements of the type: "If client says _____ , then therapist says _____ ." It involves learning a *system* of psychotherapy which includes as just one of its features the acquisition of technique.

The primary purpose of this book is to develop a means of conceptualizing psychotherapy in systematic terms and to present some ways by which this knowledge can be translated into action. Basically, this involves formulating therapy in terms of a developmental process, as a sequence of behaviorally defined stages which generate the techniques used in treatment. The first part of the book, consequently, deals with such issues as the relation of theory to practice, the meaning of psychotherapy stages, and the extent to which therapy "rules" guide the therapist's actions. My goal is to spell out as concretely as possible the theoretical and practical considerations that lead to effective therapeutic change.

The remainder of the book deals with the application of this stage framework to a particular form of psychotherapy that focuses specifically on the nature of the therapist-client relationship. Labeled "Interactional Psychotherapy," the approach addresses itself to those relational aspects of treatment that are thought to contribute most saliently to psychological change. Interactional psychotherapy represents an effort to depict the ways in which the therapist uses himself as a therapeutic tool—as a professional who allows himself to be temporarily used for the psychological benefit of others.

Although interactional therapy is presented as an integral system in its own right, it is offered as a learning tool for bridging the diverse approaches to psychotherapeutic change. The rationale for this lies in the critical role that the client-therapist relationship plays in practically every form of treatment. Thus Goldstein et al., commenting on the divergence in theory and technique that exists among the various schools of psychotherapy, conclude: "On one point, however, the degree of theoretical and operational convergence is marked, namely the centrality accorded the interpersonal relationship between the therapist and patient" (1966, p. 73). It is this consideration that underlies interactional psychotherapy and links it to other systems of behavior change.

Chapters 1 and 2 are devoted to the development of the process perspective and explore the consequences of depicting psychotherapy by means of a stage framework. In these chapters, the concept of psychotherapy rules and their relation to stages are spelled out in some detail and applied to several well-known systems of psychotherapy. In succeeding chapters, the process perspective is applied more extensively to interactional psychotherapy; Chapter 3 presents the theory underlying the interactional approach, while Chapters 4 and 5 apply the process framework to, respectively, individual and group therapy. The overall aim is to offer those who work with troubled human beings a set of relational tools with which they may approach their complex task.

I wish to thank Robert Carson, Bruce Denner, Albert Ellis, Alexandra Kaplan, and Joseph Matarazzo for reading the manuscript and making valuable suggestions. All gave generously of their time. Thanks are also due to Sally Ives and Betty Cinq-Mars; both helped in the technical preparation of the manuscript and always extended themselves in the face of deadlines and other pressures. Finally, there is my wife, Eva. Throughout the manuscript's preparation, she acted as a sounding board, critic-at-large, and a source of constant support. To her I owe more than I can express.

S. Cashdan
Amherst, Massachusetts
April, 1973

Interactional Psychotherapy

**Stages and Strategies
in Behavioral Change**

1
The Process of Psychotherapy

INTRODUCTION

Before one can meaningfully ask how to conduct psychotherapy, it is necessary to first ask what psychotherapy is. The definition of psychotherapy, however, is elusive. Surveying the different systems of psychotherapy in use today, one is able to uncover almost as many different definitions as there are systems. The widespread use of terms such as insight, transference, self-actualization, and reinforcement might lead one to conclude, moreover, that therapists are speaking of qualitatively different organisms in referring to the recipients of their help. Despite this, there are some communalities that tie the diverse approaches together.

At the very least, most approaches to psychotherapy revolve about a rather unique relationship between client and therapist. Its uniqueness lies in the fact that unlike other professional relationships (lawyer-client, physician-patient, etc.), the therapist-client relationship itself functions as the primary medium of change. Although the extent of the therapist's use of the relationship varies somewhat from system to system, it tends to be a distinct feature of treatment approaches that go under the rubric of psychotherapy.

Most definitions of psychotherapy, in addition, also embrace some notion of *behavior change*. The question of whether observable

1

change need manifest itself within the therapy session remains a moot point; that some type of new behavior must ultimately emerge, however, is usually agreed upon by most workers in the field. Even those committed to a "cognitive" interpretation of psychotherapy allow that "the final test . . . must be in the market-place" and "ultimately the client will have to engage in the practice [of social skills] to realize this benefit" (Levy, 1967, p. 22). While concepts such as insight, modified self-image, or cognitive restructuring are given a great deal of attention, some form of behavior change remains a central feature in most attempts to specify the nature of psychotherapy.

Psychotherapy, moreover, is designed to produce changes which are relatively *long-lasting*. Many therapists are capable of initiating immediate change in their patients simply by telling them how to behave or by relying on the power of modeling. But experience indicates that these effects often are shortlived and do not seem to strike at the heart of the patient's difficulties. Short-term behavioral shifts such as being nice to one's wife for a week or being occasionally assertive with a superior are not essential to a definition of psychotherapy, whereas long-term changes are.

Finally, psychotherapy is meant to produce a change in what might be called *emotional well-being*. Most prospective clients arrive in a state of emotional distress which psychotherapy attempts to alter. While some patients may indicate that they are interested in psychotherapy solely as an intellectual exercise, most therapists will eschew these individuals in favor of clients who are truly hurting. Psychotherapy is meant to reduce anxiety, alleviate depression, and salvage deteriorating relationships, rather than being a didactic exercise for the client. In sum, then, psychotherapy can be defined as a professional service designed to bring about *behavior change* that is *long-lasting* and is accompanied by an increase in *emotional well-being*.

While these criteria are somewhat broad, disordered behavior is complex and thus difficult to specify with pinpoint accuracy. Any definition of psychotherapy, therefore, will reflect this. A broad definition, nonetheless, can prove useful by prescribing the outer limits of a concept. That is to say, our tentative working definition allows us to say what is *not* psychotherapy. And psychotherapy is not: talking to a friend, taking a tranquilizer, resting for a while in a sanitarium, and other procedures which do not meet the prerequisites of the definition. Moreover, the definition becomes more precise when applied to specific systems. Thus, within a psychoanalytic framework, more flexible responses with sexual and authority figures correspond to *behavior change;* "emotional reconstruction of the personality" fulfills the *long-lasting* criterion; and the reduction of anxiety and removal of symptoms is compatible with increased *emotional well-being.*

A close look at each of the defining features of psychotherapy strongly suggests that they are not static criteria. The road from less to more adaptive social functioning is reflected in gradual changes on the part of the patient. Similarly, the change from emotional distress to emotional well-being also occurs slowly. Were this not so, psychotherapy could consist of one or two "talking sessions" during which the client simply would be told how he ought to behave. This would soon be followed by a sudden upsurge in emotional well-being. Obviously, this rarely occurs; what we witness instead are incremental longitudinal changes—changes which, when taken together, are regarded as positive or psychotherapeutic. These longitudinal changes, represented in a series of patterned patient-therapist exchanges, are what allow us to characterize psychotherapy as a *process* (Cashdan, 1967).

The word "process" is usually defined as (1) any phenomena which shows a continuous change in time and (2) a series of operations definitely leading to an end. The phrase "change in time" signifies that the events comprising psychotherapy, be they transference phenomena, catharsis, or confrontation, do not remain constant. Moreover, the term "series" suggests not only that we attend to the events per se but that special attention be devoted to their *order.* Even though it is important that a psychotherapy process dictate such diverse techniques as reinforcement or interpretation, it is even more important to know precisely where in the therapy sequence these should be invoked. Commenting on this point, Ford and Urban (1963) write:

> Some rationale about the order in which changes should be attempted is both a conceptual and procedural necessity.... [The therapist] needs some way of deciding what to respond to immediately, what to ignore, and what to defer until later; that is, he must have some notion about the order in which to proceed. (p. 686)

A psychotherapy process is essentially a miniature theory that specifies how therapist operations are sequenced. In addition, a psychotherapy process predicts what changes can be expected in the patient as the therapy progresses. A set of *therapist operations* coupled with a reliable change in the patient's behavior (*a behavioral shift*) define a psychotherapy "stage." A psychotherapy process therefore subsumes a set of stages which are defined both by therapist operations and by patient behavioral shifts. In brief, it depicts the theory of therapy in operational terms.

If the notion of stages is applied to all theories of therapy, we approach the realm of what could be considered a process theory. This general framework would spell out the formal characteristics of all psychotherapy processes by designating functional relationships among stages. When these notions are applied to a particular system, a subtheory is generated which then depicts the particular process of that approach. Thus, all therapy systems, ranging from psychoanalysis to systematic desensitization, would adhere to some general prescriptions concerning stage relationships. Any one approach would prescribe the precise number of stages in the system, their exact order, and the therapist operations associated with each.

The concept of a process framework for psychotherapy is proposed as a medium for learning the complex art of therapeutic intervention. Curiously, theoretical stage frameworks have not been generally adopted by psychotherapists even though they have proven fruitful in other areas of psychology.* Piaget's theory of development, for example, is a conceptual scheme which prescribes how the developing child's behavior can be meaningfully categorized and studied in a stage framework. Today, child psychologists argue over the order of Piaget's stages, as well as the importance of particular stages. Never-. theless, acceptance of his framework makes such discussion and sharing of ideas possible. It is proposed that a process framework for conceptualizing psychotherapy can prove similarly fruitful.

PROCESS IN PSYCHOTHERAPY

The major thesis of this book is that a stage account of psychotherapy promotes effective treatment by generating technique. From this it follows that the therapist's tactics are governed not so much by

---

* A notable exception occurs in the conceptualizations of Carl Rogers (1959, 1961).

client utterances as by a plan that transcends the specific case. Although some might reject this view and argue the need to flexibly fit the treatment to the patient (e.g., see Alexander and French, 1946), others tend to support it. Carl Rogers (1959), for example, writes:

> It has been our experience to date that although the therapeutic relationship is used differently by different clients, it is not necessary nor helpful to manipulate the relationship in specific ways for specific kinds of clients. (pp. 213-214)

This does not mean that the therapist's procedures are rigid and unyielding; in fact, many interchanges in a particular case may never be repeated with other clients. It does, however, place certain constraints on the character of the treatment process, constraints represented by stages and the operations that comprise them.

The stages of psychotherapy essentially stipulate the form a particular treatment approach will take. Within each stage are prescriptions, or *rules,* that govern the therapist's behavioral responses. Such rules generate the concrete responses of the therapist that are called *technique.* A stage, however, is composed not only of rules but of changes, or shifts, in the patient's behavior. Therapy process can therefore be defined as a series of stages, each of which is composed of a set of rules and an associated behavioral shift. This is schematically depicted in Figure 1. The input and output notations represent the "before" and "after" behaviors of the patient. In other words, they depict the behavioral shift of a particular stage.

The overall psychotherapy process theoretically depicts a series of ideal antecedent—consequent conditions designed to enact change. Operationally, it denotes a series of rules that guide the therapy in a direction the therapist considers beneficial. In order to effect change, a therapist needs to know these rules and have some idea of the sequence they follow. The various shifts in the patient's behavior and the rules that facilitate these shifts comprise the stage account of a particular psychotherapy, i.e., the system's "process."

Where does the process of psychotherapy originate? Ideally it should derive from a body of propositions concerning man's goals, aspirations, and desires—a theory of personality (Ford and Urban, 1963, p. 10). A historical survey of psychotherapy, however, suggests that just the opposite has occurred; rather than therapy process having grown out of change notions embedded in a personality theory, it has instead generated the theory!

6

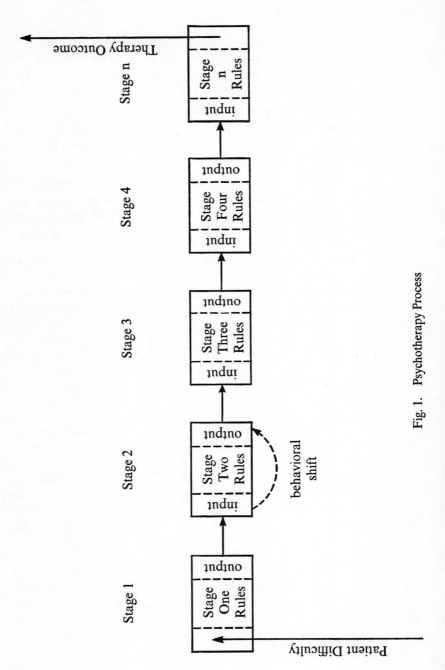

Fig. 1. Psychotherapy Process

This perhaps is one of the reasons that psychotherapy training today is conducted with a heavy emphasis on the procedure as art. In training settings, many beginning therapists are called upon to "wing it," to come up with impromptu, innovative performances that hopefully will facilitate meaningful change. Not knowing what to expect or what to accomplish in a specific session, beginning therapists are thus forced to engage in on-the-spot improvisations, the result of which is often confusion and embarrassment.

For both practical and epistemological reasons, we would hope that theory-to-process derivations could be performed. The ability to logically derive treatment from theory could not only advance the teaching of therapy but also foster insight into the inherent limitations and potentials of specific approaches. One of the potential benefits of being able to derive process from theory is that it offers psychotherapists a heuristic device for evaluating diverse approaches which lay claim to the same theoretical underpinnings.

London (1964) addresses himself to this issue in contrasting Wolpe's "systematic desensitization" with Stampfl's "implosive therapy." Essentially, Wolpe takes the view that anxiety to a very fightening stimulus or situation can be reduced by gently leading the client through similar but less frightening situations in which lower levels of anxiety are systematically extinguished (Wolpe, 1958, 1969). In contrast, Stampfl's implosive therapy involves bombarding the patient with intense anxiety experiences directly associated with those that brought him to treatment (Stampfl and Levis, 1967). London (1964) suggests that these approaches are incompatible if we expect to derive both of them from a single theoretical point of view.

> According to their theories, Stampfl must claim that Wolpe cannot get results if he is doing what he thinks he is doing (inhibiting anxiety) and Wolpe must extend Stampfl the same courtesy! (p. 107)

Only by arbitrarily defining anxiety in ways that are convenient for a particular formulation can one logically hope to extinguish it by both a spoonfeeding *and* a bombardment approach.

Even though it is desirable that a system's personality theory and therapy process be compatible, it is imperative that the process itself be internally consistent. Otherwise, psychotherapy technique is reduced to a potpourri of maneuvers and ploys guided more by patient idiosyncracies than therapist design. To provide the requisite internal

consistency for psychotherapy process, three general guidelines or
stage principles are proposed. These principles are the procedural
glue that holds the stages of a system together.

PSYCHOTHERAPY STAGE PRINCIPLES

Although the number and character of stages vary with each
therapy system, the manner by which stages are bound together
remains the same. Irrespective of the specific system under consideration, stages are related to one another by means of three invariant
functions labeled "stage principles," called *continuity, ordinality,* and
nonexclusion principles. The first deals with the behavioral relations
between adjacent stages, the second with the sequencing of stages,
and the third with stage omission.

Continuity Principle

In order to clearly describe the continuity principle, it is necessary to recall the fact that therapy rules, per se, reflect only part of the
entire therapeutic transaction. The other part is depicted by a series
of related changes in the patient; from the vantage point of a single
stage, we are speaking of an incremental shift in the patient's behavior. This shift is often depicted in acts or statements that adopt a
certain form but not necessarily a change in content. Thus, the
psychoanalytic patient may say or do a variety of things in response
to the "blank screen" of the analyst, all of which differ markedly in
content; all, however, depict a state of frustration. The reliable appearance of frustration responses, as such, defines the behavioral shift
of that stage and thus provides the signal for progression into the next
stage.

Movement of this type is governed by the continuity principle:
the behavioral shift of the client which forms the output of any one
stage comprises the input for the subsequent stage. If, then, the
purpose of a particular stage is to shift a patient's *symptom* statements to *interpersonal* statements, the rules of that stage would be
designed to do just this.* The rules of the next stage, accordingly,

---

* This might be accomplished by repeatedly focusing on whom the symptom
affects rather than on how much personal agony it evokes.

would be designed to deal only with interpersonal matters. Therefore, the therapist does not have to be particularly concerned with symptom matters once they have been dealt with in an earlier stage; if symptom statements occur, they should be ignored or viewed as transient interference. Continual intrusion of such statements, however, would point to the ineffective execution of an earlier stage and the need to backtrack. Optimally speaking, symptom statements should not appear if the preceding stage has been successfully negotiated.

A significant implication of the continuity principle is that many of the events of psychotherapy are generated by the treatment process itself. Content such as that contained in reports of current events or past reminiscences is in many instances used mainly to facilitate the development of behavioral shifts such as frustration, insight, acting out, self-disclosure, and so on. The therapist consequently need not feel that the treatment depends upon crises and problems arising in the day-to-day life of the patient.

Ordinality Principle

The second major principle addresses itself to the ordinal relation of stages, or how stages are sequenced. The ordinality principle basically proposes that the order of stages is immutable. Each stage in the psychotherapy process is fixed with relation to the stage which precedes it and the one that follows it. The therapist consequently must not change the order of stages or return to an earlier stage without retracing intervening steps. This second stage principle states, in short, that the stages of a psychotherapy process must adhere to a fixed, ordinal progression to ensure successful execution of the therapy.

A simple illustration of the ordinality principle is seen in Wolpe's systematic desensitization. As indicated earlier, Wolpe's approach involves leading the patient through a series of graded anxiety experiences that are similar to the basic phobia. These graded experiences are operationally depicted in a list called an "anxiety hierarchy." Assuming that the list is correctly ordered and complete, failure of the client to progress up the hierarchy signifies the need to return to some lower level and to retrace the intervening steps (Wolpe, 1969, p. 129). If, for example, progress is impeded at Step 8 and the patient eventually has to return to negotiate Step 5, he will have to progress once more through Steps 6 and 7 of the hierarchy. The ordinality principle, like the continuity principle, thus functions to maintain the structural integrity of the specific system under consideration.

Nonexclusion Principle

The third and final principle simply states that no stage in the process may be excluded. The nonexclusion principle is thus a logical corollary of the continuity principle. Since the rules of any one stage are designed to cope with the output of the preceding stage, omission of a stage leads to serious discontinuity.

The importance of the nonexclusion principle should not be underestimated, particularly by beginning therapists. Very often, patients paradoxically develop "insight" or report a newly acquired "ability" to cope with their problems just when the therapy begins to get stressful. If the therapist responds by either skipping a stage or engineering a premature termination, he may be rudely surprised by an exacerbation of symptoms or by the patient returning some weeks later with the same complaint. When there is any question of doubt, trust the process, not the patient.

Carl Rogers (1958), in an article describing his seven-stage conception of client-centered therapy, offers support for the presence of superordinate stage principles:

> Thus, a client who is generally at Stage 2 or 3 seems unlikely to exhibit any behaviors characteristic of Stage 5. This is especially true if we limit observations to a single defined area of related personal meaning in the client. Then I would hypothesize that there will be considerable regularity, that Stage 3 would rarely be found before Stage 2, that Stage 4 would rarely follow Stage 2 without Stage 3 intervening. (p. 146)

This excerpt clearly demonstrates the operation of the continuity and ordinality principles. Also implied is the presence of the nonexclusion principle.

The theoretical process framework introduced in the preceding pages is seen as facilitating spontaneity and innovation on the part of the therapist. By setting up general stagebound prescriptions for therapist and client, it allows maximum freedom within a stage (and with specific clients) for meeting these requirements. Thus, if we wish the patient to comprehend the negative implications of certain actions, this may be achieved via verbal interpretations with cognitive, reflective types, and by active role-playing with motoric types. Whatever course is adopted also depends on what the therapist himself feels comfortable with. In the end, however, therapeutic goals are more likely to be realized where structure facilitates technique.

The framework can also function as a rough means of validating one's treatment methods, since at one time or another every conscientious therapist must gauge his effectiveness. If each therapy is conducted in a completely unique manner, the therapist will not be able to clearly ascribe outcomes, particularly negative ones, to client variables or therapy technique. Did the client fail to improve (or did he deteriorate) because of *his* initial anxiety level or lack of "psychological mindedness," or was it because *our* interpretations were too superficial, too deep, or perhaps poorly timed? Inasmuch as we hope that not only the client but the therapist respects what he can learn from the therapy encounter, every psychotherapy should be perceived as a type of microcosmic psychological experiment—some factors change while others remain relatively constant. These constant factors make up the formal elements in the system and are subsumed under the concepts of stages and rules.

The foregoing obviously also bears on the work of the psychotherapy researcher who, generally speaking, is not concerned with the particular case so much as with the question of whether a given approach is effective or not. The once-hotly contested "outcome" question, however, has been largely abandoned in favor of more specific questions involving who is being treated by whom and by what method (Bergin, 1971; Strupp and Bergin, 1969). In the face of increasing theoretical and methodological sophistication, there is an increasing emphasis nowadays on process research, with its focus on what is going on between therapist and client.

The process-outcome distinction, however, can be misleading if taken at face value. Process and outcome are inextricably linked and to consider one outside the context of the other may be shortsighted (Kiesler, 1971). Thus, if we are concerned with "what works," we cannot simply compare patients who have terminated in system A with those terminating in system B without acknowledging that people terminate for very different reasons at different points in the treatment process. While some patients terminate because *they* feel sufficiently improved, others do so because *the therapist* feels this way, and others still because of circumstances quite external to the therapy process itself (the end of the school year, the termination of a psychiatric residency or clinical internship, etc.). A close consideration of therapeutic change suggests that such change cannot be meaningfully analyzed without considering where one is in the overall therapy process.

Although the process framework presented in this chapter offers a number of theoretical and practical advantages, its adoption is not without danger. As Yalom (1970) points out, stereotyped expectations can lead to much confusion if the novice takes the concept of developmental phases too literally. He cautions that ". . . developmental phases are rarely well demarcated; there is considerable overlap and the boundaries between them are at best dim" (p. 241). He nevertheless goes on to say:

> Despite these shortcomings, the proposed developmental sequence has much to recommend it. . . . Once the therapist has a concept of the developmental sequence, he is more easily able to maintain his objectivity and to appreciate the course the [therapy] pursues. . . . (p. 244)

Consequently, if the concept of a process framework (developmental sequence) is used judiciously, it can provide a clarity and order that the student and practitioner may find beneficial. In the next chapter we will consider how this framework is applied to the actual transactions that constitute the practice of psychotherapy.

2
The Practice of Psychotherapy

What the therapist actually does in the course of treatment is perhaps the most central concern of practitioners and students alike. While discussion of this topic almost always centers around issues of technique, consideration of technique alone presents a somewhat limited view of what actually goes on in treatment. Close attention to a specific interpretive remark, for example, sheds little light on why a therapist chooses to make this particular association at this particular time. Mere observation of his behavior, moreover, does not reveal why he attends to certain of the patient's actions and ignores others. The therapist apparently draws upon a body of knowledge, a conceptualization of the case, which is not readily available to the naive observer.

This conceptualization, referred to as the *case formulation,* comprises a set of hypotheses that assert something about the various complaints and "facts" the patient presents to the therapist. Since the patient in the course of treatment invariably comes up with new facts—and sometimes new complaints—the case formulation must be fluid and capable of assimilating new information. A thorough understanding of a therapist's technique, consequently, depends on a knowledge of the principles that guide his conceptualizations. We therefore devote some consideration to the matter of clinical formulations.

THE CASE FORMULATION

Much of our daily life involves transforming the "raw data" of sensory events and experiences into a form which can be handled effectively. Basically, transformations of this sort are guiding principles that simplify the difficult decisions that human beings encounter in their everyday transactions. Even "logic" represents a set of guidelines by which persons construe the relationships among different events; others may be predisposed to select the same events and interpret them in terms of magical ties and animism.

Generally speaking, transformations do not occur in a vacuum but derive from certain assumptions regarding the nature of man and his world. On the basis of such assumptions, some people view the interpersonal world optimistically, construing the behavior of others as benevolent and well-meaning, while others take a pessimistic view. For them, the world is potentially harmful and calls forth suspicious attitudes and cautious behavior. In between lies a variety of cognitive "models" that guide people's perceptions and influence their decisions (Lindesmith and Strauss, 1968, p. 12).

The formulative efforts of psychotherapists also tend to be based on assumptions involving the nature of man. But in the field of psychotherapy many different models of man exist. Although it is possible to subscribe to more than one model at a time, most therapists usually commit themselves to a single model since the assumptions underlying different models contain antithetical elements. Thus, anxiety over public speaking would be formulated differently by a psychoanalyst and a behavior therapist. The behaviorist, with his emphasis on reinforcement history, is likely to phrase his formulation in terms of public exposure experiences involving negative reinforcement. The psychoanalyst, rooting his formulation in assumptions regarding human sexuality, is more likely to invoke the concept of castration anxiety, especially if the patient desperately clutches the microphone.

Most students in the helping professions are initially exposed to models and their derivative guidelines in their course work. These are presented (often implicitly) in courses dealing with theories or models of personality. If the training setting is analytically oriented, students are taught to view pathological behavior in light of historical antecedents and unconscious determinants. Even though case referents may differ, in an analytic framework case conceptualizations are phrased in terms of Oedipal conflicts, repressed impulses, and psychosocial fixations. In a client-centered setting, the client's disturbed behavior is construed in terms of incongruence between "self" and "experience." Each theoretical approach thus provides its own guidelines for constructing clinical formulations. Further inspection of these formulations suggests that each contains selective and transformational components.

Selecting Data

From what has been said, it is obvious that the therapist must continually make important decisions concerning the type of material he selects in constructing his formulations. An examination of most well-known models of personality leads to the conclusion that each is best designed to handle different types of data. The psychoanalyst, consequently, is more apt to focus on historical determinants of a patient's anxiety, whereas the behavior therapist is more likely to focus upon current contributing factors. Construction of a formulation is facilitated by the selection of the type of material which the personality model manages best.

This selectivity function is demonstrated in the example of a general practitioner faced with the task of prescribing treatment for a patient who complains of severe headaches. For argument's sake, let us assume that this is an older physician who has little experience with disorders involving psychogenic factors. Following standard procedure, he first takes a medical and social history, an anamnesis, to help chart the onset and course of the patient's disorder. He finds, among other things, that the headaches fail to follow a familial pattern, that they occur fairly frequently, and that they are most bothersome during the week. He also learns that the patient's nasal passages are constantly clogged and that he suffers from air-borne allergens. Finally, he discovers that his patient is a college graduate earning $6,500 per year in a position that he has held since graduating from college almost four years ago.

A brief physical examination reveals normal pupillary reflexes but an arrhythmic breathing pattern and heightened blood pressure. With this information, he proceeds to formulate a diagnosis based on principles of systemic dysfunction, principles rooted in a biological model of human disorder. This might result in a diagnosis of chronic sinusitis complicated by an allergic condition which occasionally triggers the headaches.

We may ask, however, whether this diagnosis is based on *all* of the information elicited during the anamnesis and physical examination. A close look at the diagnostic process reveals that the physician has selectively chosen only certain material; not surprisingly, he has selected data that is easily translated into the language of the biological model to which he subscribes. This model readily accepts inputs such as locus of pain, respiration rate, blood pressure, and so on, but cannot handle information concerning achievement, anger, or conflict, or their subtle interaction with biological states. All it can do is accept a patient's bodily complaints, couple them with readings off a plethysmograph, and translate this into the language of physiomedical events—the language of vascular, muscular, and biochemical dysfunction. Given the character and capacities of this model, its operation is actually facilitated by the screening out of irrelevant and redundant material.

For the moment, we interrupt this physician's work and join him at lunch with a friend, a colleague who happens to be a psychiatrist. Since this case is fresh in his mind, he casually relates the details to his interested friend. If we were to privately interview the psychiatrist afterwards, we would most likely hear a different diagnosis. It would not surprise us under these circumstances to hear the psychiatrist render a diagnosis of tension, or perhaps even hysterical, headache.

It is obvious that both the general practitioner and the psychiatrist were exposed to the same total body of patient information; nevertheless, each arrived at a different conclusion. This can be traced to the fact that they harbor divergent conceptual models. Moreover, optimal functioning of the psychiatrist's model demands information that differs from, or at least goes beyond, the general practitioner's.

The hypothetical situation we just proposed is not too different from that which exists in the realm of psychotherapy. Looking at the various models to which therapists subscribe, we find not too surprisingly that therapists vary in their receptivity to different forms of input. The client-centered therapist is thus more likely than the behaviorist to focus on the client's self-image; the psychoanalyst is more likely than the client-centered therapist to concentrate on symbolic material such as dreams. A significant aspect of constructing formulations consequently depends upon the selection of appropriate data.

Transforming Data

Once relevant data are gathered, they are subjected to further manipulation, since straight descriptive accounts of problem behavior do not typically yield useful solutions. A close look at the activities involved in most professional services, be they psychotherapeutic, legal, or medical, usually reveals a reformulation of the client's difficulty into terms that foster effective action. The legal consequences of hitting a pedestrian are thus vastly different when construed as an act against an individual as opposed to an act against the state. In the former case, a settlement or civil suit is a likely outcome, while in the latter case a charge of criminal negligence may result. Phenomenologically similar events can, therefore, lead to radically different outcomes, depending on how the events are interpreted and who is doing the interpreting.

Returning to the two physicians introduced earlier, we would be astonished to find either prescribing help in the form of strong, directive statements. Our sense of propriety would be disturbed if the psychiatrist or general practitioner told the patient, "You shouldn't have headaches," or "Don't have any more." If this occurred, their behaviors might be labeled inappropriate, even unethical. Our response is obviously based on the discrepancy between such statements and the formulative models that we assume these physicians hold. Similar statements might be quite acceptable in the context of another model. This is evident if we monitor our reactions to the identical remarks coming from a hypnotherapist!

In psychotherapy, the material that the therapist selects from client's reports must also be translated into useable form. Essentially this involves rephrasing the client's concrete experiences and impressions into theoretical terms. This is accomplished by means of an encoding process which transforms the patient's actions and verbalizations into a new language. Thus, the patient's statement, "I am terribly afraid of heights," leads to very little in the way of meaningful help if it is accepted at face value. If, however, the symptom is construed as a conditioned avoidance response, it may prove amenable to treatment by systematic desensitization. If construed as a symbolic indication of fear over loss of ego control, it may be approached through psychoanalysis or one of its derivatives. Transformation of the phobic complaint into a theoretical language introduces a host of novel responses previously unavailable and increases the possibility of remediation.

To briefly summarize, a clinical formulation converts the language of experience into the language of theory so as to facilitate change. Just as physicians evolve disparate formulations from different models, so do psychotherapists. The formulations of therapists, however, are based on psychological rather than biological models. Once a formulation is generated, it acts to facilitate the concrete means by which the therapist exerts influence. These, of course, are the techniques of psychotherapy. We therefore turn to interpretations as well as other devices that fall under the rubric of technique.

TECHNIQUE IN PSYCHOTHERAPY

The psychotherapist, in addition to "making something" of what the patient says and does, responds to these behaviors in definable ways. Thus, at any point in the treatment process, the therapist can choose or decline to make an interpretation; he may choose, moreover, to react or not react to silences, angry outbursts, crying, etc. That is to say, certain behaviors of the therapist may be quite independent of the facts which he has accumulated about the patient.

The therapist obviously must have some basis for judging whether to interpret as well as whether to respond behaviorally. The bases for these decisions reside in rules regarding the therapist's interactional behavior; certain of these rules address themselves specifically to interpretive techniques, others to techniques such as inquisitory ploys and confrontation, and others to direct suggestions and explicit training procedures. Together, these constitute the "rules of psychotherapy."

The diverse techniques that therapists employ are governed for the most part by three different types of rules: *interpretive, reactive,* and *directive* rules. In general, the interpretive rules result in verbal statements that directly or indirectly guide the patient in the direction of explanatory associations. Reactive and directive rules encompass a variety of verbal and nonverbal reactions, ranging from suggestions to silence, that function to promote the development of desired behavioral responses on the part of the patient.

Interpretive Rules

These rules govern the association of two or more disparate events which differ along symbolic, temporal, or emotional lines.

Essentially the therapist's job is to help the patient discover the hidden relationships that tie such events together. Some associations link past and present occurrences, e.g., an unresolved Oedipal conflict and current guilt over sex. Others tie together seemingly unconnected events in the patient's contemporary life, e.g., anger toward spouse and anger toward an employer. Still others help the patient come to grips with the emotional components of "rational" intellectual decisions. An example is fear of independence underlying a decision to prolong one's stay in school or the military.

The directives contained in interpretive rules can be fulfilled in more than one way. The therapist, for one, can actually make the association for the patient via the route, "It seems to me that ..." More often, however, the patient is guided in the direction of semi-independent discoveries, e.g., "Do you see any connection between _____ and what happened to you as a child?" Experience indicates that therapists who guide the patient are usually more effective than those who simply make grand pronouncements. Whatever route is adopted, it is important that the patient be convinced of the interpretation's validity. Otherwise it will prove ineffective in promoting change.

To fully comprehend the makeup of interpretations, it is necessary to consider both their form and content. The form that an interpretation takes is prescribed by the stage in the therapy process currently being negotiated. Thus those points in the treatment process in which the therapist decides to make present to past connections or link intrasession with extrasession behaviors will tend to remain fairly constant. The question of which specific behaviors should be linked depends, of course, upon the particular case. The content of an interpretation, therefore, is quite variable.

The common interpretive rule, "associate childhood event with symptom," can consequently encompass a range of phenomena. Symptoms can range from phobias to dissociative episodes to delusional beliefs; "childhood events" may encompass such things as viewing parental intercourse, punishment for masturbation, or harboring destructive thoughts. How does the therapist know which content, which events or behaviors, to select? It is evident that the answer to this question is not contained within the interpretive rule but in the formulation.

The case formulation is the repository for the content used in interpretations. By the time interpretations are introduced in the treatment process, the formulation typically is quite complete. Incorrect hypotheses have long since been discarded and the remaining material modified and refined to produce a fairly accurate picture of the events in the patient's life that are meaningfully related. Feeling fairly confident about the accuracy of the material at his disposal, the therapist is thus able to choose the inputs that will comprise the content of interpretive interventions. Successful interpretive technique therefore entails little more than judicious integration of formulative content with interpretive rules.

Interpretations, in sum, contain both form and content elements. The form is prescribed by interpretive rules, while the content emerges from the clinical formulation. Just as formulations are uniquely tied to individual cases, interpretive rules are a function of the therapy system within which one operates. We therefore defer more detailed consideration of interpretive rules until specific approaches are discussed.

Reactive Rules

Although popular conceptions of psychotherapy portray treatment solely in interpretive terms, experienced therapists recognize this conception for the myth it is. The story of the patient who enters therapy and is cured via profound interpretations is little more than a literary device. Therapies that are exclusively interpretive, in fact, often result in intellectualized "cures" and little behavioral change. Much of what transpires in psychotherapy therefore revolves about noninterpretive means of dealing with the patient.

By noninterpretive techniques, we are speaking of such things as subtle inquiries, direct challenges, bodily gestures, facial expressions, and silences. All these techniques are generated by devices called reactive rules, some examples being: do not gratify the patient, accept patient harassment, confront patient, etc. In contrast to interpretive rules, reactive rules do not contain content elements, but simply take the form of behavioral prescriptions. Like interpretive rules, however, they can be satisfied in more than one way. Thus, the reactive rule, "confront the patient," can be satisfied by a direct verbal challenge, a quizzical expression, or some other response. The choice of a specific technique always remains the prerogative of the therapist.

Reactive rules play an important and pervasive role in practically every system of psychotherapy. A brief survey of the changes that occur within divergent approaches reveals movement along such dimensions as regression, self-disclosure, organismic valuing, and so on. Close examination reveals that movement of this sort is often facilitated not so much by interpretations as by the reactions of the therapist. Thus, regression in psychoanalytic treatment is achieved not through intellectual analysis but through the therapist's refusal of the patient's requests for support and explanation. The "abstinence rule" which dictates this response is a reactive rule (Menninger, 1958, p. 56). In client-centered treatment, movement is fostered through unconditional positive regard, also a reactive rule, rather than through attempts to link the patient's present "experiencing" with events in the past.

The operation of reactive rules is often apparent in the beginning phases of treatment. In most systems, the first stage is usually devoted to soliciting information needed for the formulation. The reactive rule of this stage, therefore, simply directs the therapist to elicit pertinent material from the patient. The specific techniques used to meet this requirement are subsumed under the label of "interview skills."

Interview skills, though they may take different forms, tend to be shared by the majority of psychotherapists regardless of therapeutic persuasion. Most therapists are quite adept, for example, at employing feigned misunderstanding; statements such as, "I don't quite understand" and quizzical expressions represent reactive means of encouraging elaboration and deeper explorations. Another common interview technique involves alternately posing questions with the terms "feel" and "mean" in them. These are strategically placed in the interview so that the patient's responses will contain both emotional and intellectual elements. This is demonstrated in the following excerpt:

> *Pt:* I put off coming for help for a long time.
> *Th:* What does that *mean* to you?
> *Pt:* (*pause*) I guess that I was afraid to admit I was sick.
> *Th:* How do you *feel* now that you're admitting it?
> *Pt:* (*pause*) Scared.
> *Th:* Scared?
> *Pt:* Scared that maybe I'm crazy.
> *Th:* What does that *mean* to you?
> *Pt:* (*grinning*) That I'll have to be put away.

Th: You seem to have some *feeling* about that.
Pt: Now that I've actually said it, it seems kind of silly.

As one can see, an entire interview can be conducted simply through the judicious use of "feeling" and "meaning" comments—comments which in turn are generated by a reactive inquiry rule. Reactive rules, in sum, generate one significant type of therapist behavior that falls outside the realm of interpretation.

Directive Rules

The third major kind of rules which guide the therapist's interventions are referred to as directive rules. Like interpretive and reactive rules, directive rules prescribe how the therapist should respond under specific circumstances. However, in this case, they direct the therapist to direct the patient!

Directive rules generally predominate in those forms of treatment where change depends on the therapist's ability to get the patient to respond in a concrete, circumscribed fashion. Whenever one finds a therapist training, teaching, commanding, or in other ways tutoring the patient in how to behave, one can be fairly sure that the therapist's behavior is being guided by directive rules.

Examples of the kinds of techniques that derive from directive rules are seen in the work of Jay Haley and Albert Ellis. Haley, in a form of treatment aptly named Directive Therapy (1963), describes a set of techniques called *paradoxical injunctions* which are designed to get the patient to immediately alter his behavior. According to Haley, much of what is considered psychopathology actually represents pathological communication patterns in which the patient acts symptomatically while simultaneously denying that he has control over his behavior. The task of the therapist is to force the patient to respond in such a way that he can no longer deny that his actions are outside of his control (Cashdan, 1972, p. 121-125).

The therapist forces the patient to respond by commanding the patient to behave in ways that are incompatible with his claims of personal impotence. Such commands, or paradoxical injunctions, typically involve telling the patient to do what he is already doing, that is, to engage in precisely the type of pathological behavior that brought him into treatment. By "prescribing the symptom," Haley claims that the patient is forced into a therapeutic double bind: if he maintains his symptom, the patient is following the therapist's command and therefore cannot claim that he cannot control what he does; if he gives up his symptom he is, de facto, "cured." Whatever the outcome, it is clear that Haley's operations are dictated by directive rules.

Rational-Emotive Therapy also relies heavily on directive techniques, but for somewhat different reasons. According to Ellis (1962), the difficulties that people experience stem from their unwillingness or inability to avoid thinking irrational thoughts. Such thoughts originate in equally unreasonable assumptions about oneself, such as, "Everyone should love me," "I should be an unqualified success," or "I should never feel anxious or depressed." The job of the therapist is to show the patient how irrational such thoughts are and to teach him how to think about things in more realistic ways.

To do this, Ellis insists that the therapist must assume an active teaching role. He must show the patient how to rethink conclusions, how to examine personal assumptions, and how to substitute a more rational philosophy of life for the one that has been getting him into difficulty. In the process, the therapist often tutors the patient in certain forms of behavior, even providing him with "homework" to insure that he practices what he is taught. In Ellis's words, "The therapist encourages, persuades, cajoles, and occassionally even insists that the patient engage in some activity (such as doing something he is afraid of doing) which itself will serve as a forceful counterpropaganda agency against the nonsense he believes" (Ellis, 1962, p. 94-95). Whether or not one agrees with Ellis's point of view or with his techniques, it is patently clear that much of what constitutes his form of psychotherapy can be codified in directive rules.

The use of directive rules is not restricted to the two approaches just discussed. It should be apparent that much of what falls under the rubric of behavior therapy is comprised of techniques that derive from rules of this sort. Thus, manipulating "social reinforcement contingencies" often involves little more than telling a mother not to respond to the temper tantrums of her recalcitrant child, or tutoring a shy individual in how to be more assertive. Whenever the therapist construes his role in terms of behavioral or cognitive re-education, the chances are that directive rules will play a significant role in the change process.*

Whether we are speaking of interpretive, reactive, or directive rules, we are calling attention to the fact that psychotherapy consists largely of therapist manipulations conducted in the service of change. While some would argue against adopting this perspective, claiming that it produces antitherapeutic attitudes on the part of the therapist, there are others who decry the relative lack of emphasis on technique:

> One wonders why [psychotherapy] theorists as a group have specified so little in the way of principles and techniques for producing behavioral change. ... A patient goes to a therapist precisely because he cannot modify his own behavior. By accepting a patient for treatment, a therapist implicitly agrees that some outside intervention is essential, and thus implicitly accepts responsibility for performing some manipulations intended to achieve behavioral change. (Ford and Urban, 1963, p. 667-668)

The authors go on to say:

> "Successful therapy" is likely to occur when the therapist is explicitly aware of the changes he wants to effect, and skillfully applies specific procedures to effect them. *Each time a therapist responds to the patient, he is implicitly or explicitly making a judgment that his responses may produce certain results at that point in time.* (p. 681)

The rules outlined in this chapter, accordingly, are designed to score the underlying principles that are responsible for these responses.

In sum, rules represent a series of internalized guidelines used to generate psychotherapy technique. Embedded in stages, rules produce the concrete responses that help the therapist achieve his goals. The beginning therapist must nevertheless be careful not to apply rules in too rigid a fashion. Greenson (1967), writing on psychoanalytic technique, remarks:

> ... rules are meant not to be commands or laws but rather guideposts which indicate the general direction. All rules have to be used elastically. ... One can reach the same goal by taking

---

* This does not mean that directive rules are tied exclusively to behavioristic approaches. The first stage of classical psychoanalysis, for example, largely entails *training* the patient how to free-associate.

bypaths and detours, but on a long journey it is of practical importance to keep in mind a road map. . . . (p. 137)

Psychotherapy is a sort of journey, and the stages and rules that make up its map can prove of inestimable value when one feels uncertain or lost.

In the remainder of this chapter, we will try to show how the concepts of psychotherapy stages and rules can be used advantageously. To show this, we will focus on psychoanalysis, behavior therapy, and brief treatment techniques, demonstrating how each can be construed in process terms. Because of their widespread use and the fact that they represent rather diverse approaches to treatment, these three methods offer a reasonable test of the process perspective.

PROCESS IN PSYCHOANALYSIS

Psychoanalysis is basically a procedure designed to enable a patient to deal more effectively with unconscious, unacceptable wishes which produce guilt, somatic symptoms, and disruptions in interpersonal functioning. Since unconscious thought processes are, by definition, outside the patient's awareness, the treatment procedure must include a device through which these impulses can become conscious. This device is the transference neurosis, an artificial illness induced in the course of treatment which sees the patient's "symptom neurosis" (his intrapsychic illness) transformed into an extrapsychic, or "interpersonal neurosis." Psychoanalysis accordingly refers to a treatment procedure in which the major emphasis revolves around the creation and subsequent resolution of a transference neurosis.

Psychoanalysis can be described by a six-stage treatment process, the interior stages of which are most intimately concerned with the development of the transference neurosis. The stages are listed below, with Stages Three and Four denoting the part of the process in which this "neurosis" is manifested most clearly.

Stage One: Free-association
Stage Two: Procedure Frustration
Stage Three: Regression (Transference Neurosis)
Stage Four: Transference Insight
Stage Five: Insight Proper
Stage Six: Working Through

Aside from some minor variations, most patients who opt for psycho-analytic treatment will have to travel through these stages.

The psychoanalytic process formally begins with the analytic client, the analysand, carefully tutored in a novel form of discourse called "free association." In Stage One, the analysand is instructed to talk about anything that comes to mind, disregarding preconceived ideas or convictions about what he thinks the analyst wants to hear. He is asked not to censor anything but to report all his thoughts (sentence fragments, memory traces, visual images, etc.), even if they seem foolish, trivial, or obscene.

Free association is basically a one-way form of communication that exposes one's private thoughts and fantasies by eliminating the restrictions normally imposed by logic, syntax, and social inhibition. Since it is a form of discourse that does not come easily to most people, the first stage of psychoanalysis is devoted to training the patient in free-associative techniques. The basic rule of this stage simply directs the analyst to teach the patient to communicate via stream-of-consciousness verbalizations and to do so without the benefit of feedback.* When the therapy hour is fully taken up by this unique, monologic form of discourse, the goal of Stage One has been reached and the stage comes to an end.

The free-associative procedure, characterized interpersonally as a "tell all—no feedback" transaction, continues smoothly until the patient begins to react specifically to the *procedure* he is being subjected to. As he obediently reveals his innermost fears, desires, and secrets, he begins to expect something in return. Feedback? Improvement in his condition? Approval from the analyst? All these and perhaps even more. However, none of these are forthcoming and, as a result, the patient begins to feel frustrated.

As months go by, this frustration grows. Throughout this time, the analyst steadfastly remains relatively unresponsive. And this is by design. The psychoanalytic process depends upon a controlled regression for its success, and this can only be achieved by calculatingly frustrating the patient. No matter what tactic the patient adopts, the psychoanalyst must deliberately withhold emotional support; aside from providing minor clarifications and reiterating the need to continue with the procedure, he remains noncommittal.

---

* If, in fact, the potential analysand finds it impossible to master these techniques, he may be judged unsuitable for psychoanalysis.

The therapy rule that underlies the analyst's deprivational attitude is referred to as the "rule of abstinence." This reactive rule essentially directs the therapist to abstain from fulfilling the patient's infantile needs. Theoretically, the abstinence rule acts to frustrate the patient's quest for neurotic gratification and results in the regression that is the earmark of psychoanalytic treatment. On an interactional level, it results in the analyst's persistent refusal to provide the patient with encouragement and support.

The patient, not too surprisingly, responds negatively to all this and starts to behave in ways that disrupt the therapy. He "forgets" certain material, avoids sensitive matters, pays his bills late, and may even "accidentally" miss appointments. It is in this stage of treatment that we first witness the unconscious efforts of the patient to block the treatment process. The painful conflict that gave rise to the patient's illness in the first place and was repressed now manifests itself in attempts to undermine the psychoanalysis.

One of the most illuminating discoveries that Freud made in his work was that a great many patients paradoxically seemed bent on sabotaging the treatment process. Freud consequently proposed that unconscious forces existed to forestall change and labeled these *resistances*. Generally speaking, resistances mark the presence of repression in the psychoanalysis. Precipitated by the frustration of the current interaction, but with roots in more basic, early frustrations, they are the patient's symbolic way of declaring that despite his avowed wish to get better, he is fearful of taking the necessary risks.

Much of Stage Two, procedure frustration, involves analyzing the patient's resistance so that the treatment process may progress. The second rule of Stage Two, an intrepretive rule, requires the therapist to analyze the patient's resistances. This is generally accomplished by interpreting defenses before content and ego before id (Greenson, 1967). In other words, the analyst must first make alterations in the forces responsible for the resistance, forces represented in ego's defenses, before he can deal with the dangerous content contained in the id. Once the patient begins to recognize how the various roadblocks he sets up are dictated by unconscious forces, the analysis can tentatively move on.

As the analysis continues on its inexorable course, the patient still tries to solicit support and encouragement. His neurotic needs have not been met and he intensifies his efforts. Despite this, he continues to meet with failure, and his frustration mounts. Eventually, genetically archaic patterns of responding to frustration, patterns overlayed by years of socialization, begin to emerge. These regressive means of coping with frustration are the precursors of the transference. While there is no clearcut point that marks the initiation of the transference neurosis, the patient's repeated attempts to solve his conflict via increasingly primitive means indexes the beginning of Stage Three.

The transference neurosis constitutes the major phenomenon of Stage Three and subsumes a series of patient-therapist interactions in which the patient interpersonally acts out his disorder. Briefly, this "neurosis" describes a series of interchanges in which the patient unwittingly casts the therapist into the role of a parental figure, and in so doing, symbolically recapitulates the circumstances under which sexual wishes were frustrated in childhood. On a behavioral level, the transference neurosis is represented in extreme compliance, childlike dependence, angry outbursts, and blatant seductivity. On a theoretical level, such behavior represents the culmination of a regressive process in which the patient comes to re-experience the frustration that marred his early years.

The rule that precipitates the development of such behavior is none other than the abstinence rule. Existing as a pervasive directive throughout almost the entire psychoanalysis, it fosters the growth of the regressive intrapsychic process that was initiated in Stage Two. By adhering to the rule of abstinence, the therapist forces the process to culminate in the phenomenon called the transference neurosis.

As the transference neurosis develops, symptoms often lessen in severity and sometimes may even disappear; this is another way of saying that the "transference neurosis" is substituted for the "symptom neurosis." When the psychotherapeutic interaction is fully characterized by this new "illness" and when the energy invested in the symptom is fully invested in the therapist, the patient's intrapsychic disorder has finally been transformed into one that is interpersonal in nature. The repressed conflict that underlies the patient's illness has been lured into the open and now can be subjected to analysis. Stage Three ends with the psychoanalytic regression, the transference neurosis, in full bloom.

The fourth stage of psychoanalysis, transference insight, involves a headlong attack on the distortions that underlie the transference neurosis. Although interpretations have been employed in Stage Two to counter resistances, they now are relied upon heavily as a means of dealing with the patient's interpersonal distortions. In the midst of an intense, protracted struggle, the analyst attempts to persuade the patient that his behaviors are really not based on anything the analyst has said or done but on events that occurred in the patient's early years.

The rule that acts to promote this insight directs the analyst to uncover causal connections between the patient's current reactions to the therapist and similar reactions to some significant figure in the past. Basically, this means tracing the antecedents of transference phenomena by repeatedly posing the question, "Toward whom did you feel this way in the past?" (Greenson, 1967, p. 313). The historical origins of transference reactions are thereby teased out of the unconscious and brought into awareness. The basic goal of treatment—making conscious what is unconscious—is thus largely accomplished in this stage.

Insight into the true nature of transference phenomena is facilitated by the fact that the analyst has maintained a noncontributory or "blank-screen" stance throughout the treatment process. The analyst has deliberately taken pains not to instigate or gratify the patient's requests. As a result, the responsibility for wish-laden transference behavior can now be squarely placed on the patient. By consistently pointing out to the patient that his behavior is not in response to anything the analyst has said or done, the analyst forces the patient to search elsewhere for the determinants of his unreasonable, infantlike demands.

This search ultimately leads, as we have just seen, to unresolved frustrations and to recognition of their historical antecedents. As the patient's unconscious wishes are exposed and the relationship between childhood phenomena and in-the-room phenomena are made clear, positive forces begin to gain an upper hand. The presence of a definite shift in the patient's behavior is described by Menninger (1958): "After a time ... the process of regression is reversed, the patient begins to grow up again. ... Infantile objectives are given up for more realistic and mature ones and the techniques likewise undergo a progressive modification in the direction of maturity" (p. 125-126). This shift marks the successful completion of Stage Four and the need to move on to the next stage in the treatment process.

Once the patient acknowledges the relevance of early erotic attachments and their transmutation within therapy, he can begin to explore his disorder more fully. Stage Five is basically designed to extricate the therapy from its narrow transference format and to relate it once more to events in the patient's contemporary life. This goal, labeled "insight proper," refers to a process in which the patient is taught to search out equivalencies between three sorts of related phenomena: (1) early childhood events, (2) in-the-therapy (transference) phenomena, and (3) contemporary events. Whereas in Stage Four the patient was helped to uncover hidden meanings and desires embedded in his transference interactions—i.e., the links between (1) and (2)—in Stage Five he is given the opportunity to see how all this relates to contemporary behavior. The final rule of psychoanalysis thus is an elaboration of the interpretive rule of Stage Four. Labeled "insight proper," it merely adds the category of "contemporary phenomena" to whatever associations were already made between early childhood and transference phenomena.

In the final or "working through" stage of psychoanalysis, the insight developed in Stage Five is used to illuminate additional trouble areas in the patient's life. This, however, requires no new technique; it merely involves application of the "insight-proper" rule to a variety of different content areas. In Stage Six, the interpretive rule of Stage Five is applied to strife-torn interactions with employers, conflicts with one's spouse, overly close attachments to same-sex friends, and so on, until the insights gained through interpretation extend into the farthest reaches of the patient's life. As the patient examines his behavior in diverse contexts via the insight process, he gains practice in this technique and incorporates it into his behavior as an ingrained habit or cognitive style.

Assuming a successful progression through all the previous stages, the working-through period comprises a successive pulling-out operation by the analyst. As content area after content area is explored, the therapist encourages the patient to take more of the interpretive responsibility on his own shoulders. Most analysts, in fact, maintain that the successful completion of psychoanalytic treatment is synonymous with continued "self-analysis." Thus, the end of psychoanalysis is marked not so much by the loss of a symptom but by adoption of a scheme through which intrapsychic and interpersonal phenomena can be profitably interpreted. This, in turn, is thought to lead to a more productive and gratifying lifestyle.

This capsule summary of classical psychoanalysis is obviously not meant to capture all the subtleties of psychoanalytic technique. Nor is it meant to advance the merits of psychoanalysis as a treatment method. It is designed merely to show how one rather unique form of psychotherapy can be described in terms of discrete stages— that is, in terms of circumscribed techniques on the part of the therapist and associated behavioral shifts on the part of the patient.

Before ending this discussion of psychoanalysis, we should point out that the process just described is highly specific to classical, or orthodox, psychoanalysis. Most of the treatment techniques in use today that are based on psychoanalytic principles fall under the rubric of "analytically-oriented" therapy. In these procedures, the process we described is drastically altered. The frustration and transference stages which constitute an integral part of the orthodox process are almost entirely omitted. The result is a treatment process based more on rational discussion and advice-giving that tends to focus on events taking place outside of, rather than within, the immediate treatment context. We will return to the topic of action-oriented analytic therapies later in discussing brief treatment techniques.

In the treatment process to which we turn next, even less attention is given to the nature of the patient-therapist interaction. The emphasis in behavior therapy is simply the direct and immediate alteration of pathological response patterns. There are, however, many different types of behavior therapies, each of which differs from the other as much as analytically-oriented therapy differs from orthodox psychoanalysis. To simply matters, we will therefore concentrate on the treatment process that perhaps most readers are familiar with: Wolpe's systematic desensitization.

PROCESS IN BEHAVIOR THERAPY

The theory underlying systematic desensitization is that anxiety responses (rapid breathing, tremors, cold sweats, etc.) have been regularly associated with, or "bonded" to, certain phobic stimuli. These stimuli, whether occurring in the form of specific objects (animal or insect phobias) or situations (fear of heights or open spaces), regularly result in anxiety. The therapist's task, simply stated, is to weaken these bonds. This task's success rests on the assumption that associative bonds can be weakened by substituting other behaviors for the anxiety responses. This diminishes the strength of the associations so that eventually anxiety no longer appears as a dominant response in the phobic situation (Wolpe, 1958, 1969).

The therapist employs two basic devices to facilitate this change—a relaxation training procedure, and an anxiety hierarchy. Relaxation training involves teaching patients to breathe deeply, relax their torso and limbs, slacken facial muscles, etc. These responses are chosen to act as the substitute behaviors because of their accessibility and simplicity in training. Successful substitution is a first step towards therapeutic success, since it is impossible to be both anxious and relaxed at the same time.

The other device, the anxiety hierarchy, is a list of objects or situations which approximate the phobic stimuli. These are ordered in such a way as to make any step in the hierarchy more anxiety-inducing than the one preceding it. Thus, the hierarchy progresses in graded steps from mild to high anxiety levels, the latter involving situations or objects which more closely resemble the phobic situation.

Systematic desensitization begins with training the patient in relaxation techniques so that relaxation responses can be produced on cue. This usually takes five or six sessions. The patient is then asked to vividly imagine the lowest step on the hierarchy. If anxiety is experienced at any time, he is told to respond by calling forth the relaxation responses he has been taught. This continues until he no longer feels anxious. The patient then progresses to the next level where the procedure is carried out once again. A successful treatment sees the patient mastering the complete hierarchy and able to face the phobic situation in reality without panic (Wolpe, 1969, p. 100).

To illustrate this procedure, imagine a patient who has approached a behavior therapist for help with a pervasive fear of flying. After some minor matters such as meeting time, fees, etc., have been taken care of, the therapy formally commences. The therapist begins by collecting as much material as he can in order to accurately reconstruct the conditions under which anxiety occurs. Much of the first few sessions is spent gathering the information that will be used to construct the anxiety hierarchy. A hierarchy for "flying phobia," ordered from least to most anxiety provoking, might look something like the following:

1. Reading a story about flying
2. Watching a plane in flight
3. Planning a trip by air
4. Buying tickets in an airport

5. Sitting in a taxiing jet plane
6. Airborne in a jet plane

The reader might keep in mind that the patient is not actually called upon to *do* these things. Instead, he is asked to *imagine* doing them. Similar hierarchies would be constructed for other patients who are fearful of flying. The precise items and their order, however, depend upon the specific case (Lang, 1964, p. 41).

After the hierarchy is constructed, the patient is trained in the various relaxation procedures. This often requires a number of sessions, since many phobic patients not only have irregular respiratory patterns but extremely tense musculature. Upon successful completion of this phase, the therapist introduces the patient to the first step on the anxiety hierarchy—reading a story about flying. The journey "up the ladder" now begins.

Over the course of subsequent sessions, the therapist guides the patient through the hierarchy toward the goal of helping him successfully negotiate the uppermost step. At each rung of the ladder, he is instructed to substitute relaxation responses whenever he begins feeling tense. As indicated, this involves relaxation of body and facial muscles, taking slow, deep breaths, and so on. The criterion for graduating to the next higher step of the hierarchy is the patient's report that he no longer feels anxious (Wolpe, 1969, pp. 121-127).

Little by little, the patient is brought up the ladder, each time learning to relax under more difficult circumstances. Eventually he reaches the top and can encounter the phobic object (at least, an imaginal representation of it) without feeling nervous. When this is accomplished, the patient is considered cured. It is assumed, of course, that the patient could actually fly without fear after completing the treatment. Otherwise, he has spent considerable time and money merely learning how to engage in courageous daydreaming.

Let us now try to unravel the foregoing account by separating the changes occurring in the patient (the behavioral shifts) from the rules the therapist follows in effecting these shifts. The former can be outlined in the following manner:

1. Patient provides anamnestic material.
2. Patient learns relaxation techniques.
3. Patient learns to substitute relaxation for anxiety responses in imaginal context of disturbing stimuli.

4. Procedure continues until patient reports significant reduction of anxiety.
5. Patient advances to next step of hierarchy.
6. Patient repeats steps 3, 4, and 5 in context of more anxiety-inducing stimuli (next step on hierarchy).
7. Patient reports disappearance of severe anxiety reaction in original phobic situation and terminates.

By delineating the treatment in this manner, one can note the sequential character of behavioral shifts. It might be parenthetically noted that certain theoretical changes are thought to occur even though they cannot be observed. For example, it is assumed that the internal, associative bonds joining stimuli to anxiety are weakened somewhere between steps 3 and 4. It is important to remember, however, that each stage is indexed by concrete changes in the patient's behavior.

The course of treatment can also be described in terms of the rules the therapist follows:

1. Obtain detailed description of phobic reactions and associated situations that result in anxiety.
   1a. Construct anxiety hierarchy.
2. Instruct patient in relaxation techniques.
3. Instruct patient to imagine first scene on hierarchy and to invoke relaxation techniques when necessary.
4. No therapist action required except for occasional reiteration of step 3.
5. Introduce next step of hierarchy.
6. Repeat steps 3, 4, and 5, etc., etc.
7. No therapist action required except for minor reinforcing remarks.

The concrete techniques that derive from such rules are closely related to, and in fact, are largely responsible for, the patient's shifts.

Matching this progression with the preceding account leads to construction of the system's process. Systematic desensitization therefore consists of some initial stages dealing with hierarchy construction and relaxation training, followed by a number of stages that deal with the different anxiety situations on the hierarchy. The stages at the end of the process reiterate the central stages of the process; although their content differs, they contain similar operations.*

We might reflect in passing that the techniques employed by the therapist occur in some ordered fashion, e.g., the therapist does not train the patient in relaxation techniques anywhere along the line but only at a certain point. In addition, adjacent stages intermesh so that each is behaviorally juxtaposed on the next. Such "constraints" correspond respectively to the ordinality and continuity principles discussed in Chapter One.

Constraints of this sort, however, do not interfere with the therapist's spontaneity or ingenuity. If, for example, a patient experiences a great deal of difficulty verbalizing phobic reactions, the therapist can deal with this in one of many different ways. He may wish to implement step 1 by having the patient write a personal account of his phobic experiences, or by getting this information from relatives, or by simply following the patient around. Rule 1 only specifies that one elicit a detailed description of the circumstances under which the phobic response occurs.

Flexibility, on the other hand, does *not* permit omission of stages or modification of their order. It would be illogical for the therapist to engage in step 3—instructing the patient to invoke relaxation procedures—without first executing steps 1 and 2. Violation of stage principles only erodes and eventually annihilates the therapy process.

The important point to keep in mind is that the genesis of technique is the process; consequently, major alterations in technique require major revisions of the process. Were this not so, it would not be feasible to extract rhyme or reason from any therapist's work with his patients; neither would it be possible to compare the work of different therapists or, for that matter, different systems. And if this is the case, "psychotherapy becomes a mystique, not teachable, not learnable, but given" (Small, 1971, p. 56).

By drawing on psychoanalysis and systematic desensitization as examples, I have tried to demonstrate the advantage of portraying psychotherapy in terms of stages. Although stage frameworks are not frequently found in the literature, there have been occasional at-

---

* The situation wherein operations in a stage or adjacent stages act in identical fashion on differing content is referred to as "looping" and also appears in other therapy systems. An example was seen in the "working-through" stage of psychoanalysis.

tempts to use them to describe the ongoing events of psychotherapy. Sullivan's (1970) depiction of the "psychiatric interview," a four-stage process consisting of formal inception, reconnaissance, detailed inquiry, and termination, is one example. Another is the seven-stage sequence developed by Rogers (1961) to portray client-centered treatment. In his conceptualization, Rogers charts the client's movement from a position of fixity to changingness, from unowned and unexpressed feelings to feelings accepted as one's own, and from fear of relationships to freedom in interaction. Although Rogers speaks of "conditions for change" rather than "rules," it is clear that the socio-emotional stances which the nondirective therapist adopts to promote movement in the client (unconditional positive regard, empathy, receiving, etc.) are fully compatible with the concept of reactive rules. It is consequently my belief that process frameworks can be developed for most existing forms of psychotherapy.

One form of psychotherapy that has gained increasing attention in the past few years is *brief psychotherapy*. Sometimes referred to as *emergency psychotherapy* or *crisis intervention,* the term encompasses a number of treatment modalities in which the major consideration is the amount of time expended. In the remainder of this chapter, we will try to see whether the process perspective outlined in the preceding pages can be profitably applied to short-term treatment techniques.

PROCESS IN BRIEF PSYCHOTHERAPY

While interest in brief psychotherapy has burgeoned in the past decade due, in part, to the growing community mental health movement and to such pragmatic considerations as the mental health manpower shortage, short-term treatment methods have been in evidence for a number of years. As early as 1951, surveys indicated that a great many of the patients treated in psychiatric clinics were seen for fewer than ten sessions (Mensh and Golden, 1951; Garfield and Kurz, 1952). Controlled studies in the 1960s, moreover, documented the effectiveness of short-term treatment (Muench, 1965; Schlien et al., 1962). Matarazzo concluded his 1965 Annual Review article on psychotherapeutic processes with the observation:

The fact is that the majority of patients seen in any given week are typically seen for a grand total of fewer than ten sessions. . . . The general practicing psychotherapist treats on a continuing basis only a few patients for as long as a year, two, three, or longer. The majority of his patients are referred to him by their physician, attorney, school, employer, the courts, welfare, and other governmental and public agencies, or by other patients, and are typically referred for personal, marital, school or occupational dysfunctions which rarely are totally incapacitating. Such patients cannot afford, nor do they expect or wish, other than a few consultation sessions. (p. 218)

If we add to this population the tremendous number of patients who are seen in community mental health clinics, outpatient clinics of psychiatric hospitals, and university mental health services, we can appreciate the ubiquitous nature of brief psychotherapy.

What precisely is brief psychotherapy? In our discussion of psychoanalysis, mention was made of analytically-oriented psychotherapies, variants of the orthodox process in which the transference stages are omitted. Even though theoretical allegiance to psychoanalytic principles is maintained, a greater emphasis is placed on advice-giving and on events taking place outside rather than inside the treatment context. Much of what is referred to as psychoanalytically-oriented psychotherapy could be seen as falling under the rubric of brief psychotherapy (Lewin, 1970; Wolberg, 1965).

But brief psychotherapy encompasses more than just analytically-oriented approaches and techniques. Small, in a book entitled *The Briefer Psychotherapies* (1971), lists no less than 73 short-term interventions, among them behavioral techniques (assertive training, counterconditioning), interpersonal techniques (confrontation, support, advice-giving), and even "placebo." Considering the diversity among the various brief psychotherapies, can common characteristics be found that distinguish them from more extended forms of treatment?

A close look at the different approaches suggests several avenues of departure. One is the *limited goals* set out for treatment; whether we are speaking of symptom removal, reversal of current distress, or resolving a crisis in a family, there is a concentrated *focus* on a particular problem. Another distinguishing characteristic is *time-limitation:* therapists who engage in brief psychotherapy often preset the end of treatment as a means of mobilizing both the client's and their own energies. Finally, the brief psychotherapies appear to adopt a *health orientation;* specific treatment techniques tend to emphasize such factors as awareness, adaptability, and coping skills rather than personal deficits or disability (Caplan, 1964, p. 83).

Underlying all this, of course, is the assumption of an *active psychotherapist.* The brief psychotherapist engages the client, prescribes "homework," and even goes so far as to engage in environmental interventions if he believes that altering the balance of social forces will prove beneficial. The passive, nonassertive, "wait-out-the-patient" stance associated with extended treatment is incompatible with brief approaches to treatment.

Reviewing the literature on brief psychotherapy, one is struck by the innovativeness that abounds in the area. Specific interventions seem to be guided more by pragmatic considerations than by theory. Is it possible, therefore, to construct a stage framework for the brief psychotherapies? Matarazzo (1971) addresses himself to this point by asking, "How much uniform following of a model based on Freud, Rogers, et al., or on 'learning theory' can a practitioner do in a mere five hours?" (p. 385). Probably very little if one's stage formulations are timebound, that is, if Stage One must take a minimum of five or six sessions, Stage Two the same, and so on. Reviewing the superordinate stage principles set forth in Chapter One, however, reveals no such constraint; though it probably occurs infrequently, it is theoretically possible to pass through an entire developmental sequence of stages within one psychotherapy session. Sullivan's (1970) conceptualization of the four stages that make up his "psychiatric interview," for example, clearly stipulates that these stages may evolve over a series of interviews, or within a single session.

Many workers in the area of brief therapy, interestingly, have attempted to conceptualize their interventions in process terms. Perhaps the need to be effective in a short period of time forces the therapist to make his operations more explicit. Thus, Fenichel (1954), operating within a psychoanalytic context, delineates a three-stage brief psychotherapy process consisting of a psychodiagnostic phase, an intervention selection phase, and an application phase. Bellak and Small (1965) extend this process somewhat, adding a working-through and termination stage; their additions seem to be addressed primarily to the issue of generalization. Finally, Klein and Lindemann (1961), operating out of a preventive intervention model, propose a four-phase scheme which bears some similarity to the ones described above but which introduces a social intervention phase. In this phase, active efforts are made to restore equilibrium in the client's existing social groups and to remove obstacles to the development of new relationships.

Distilling what these and other theorists have to say about brief psychotherapy, it seems that a general process account might take the following form:

Relationship Stage
Analysis Stage
Planning Stage
Implementation Stage

The *relationship stage,* generally speaking, would involve attempts to quickly form a therapeutic alliance. Within this stage, the therapists's task is to get the client to regard him with a modicum of trust in as short a time as possible. In some instances this might mean establishing rapport through the creation of a friendly nonprofessional atmosphere, while in others it might mean accentuating the therapist's status as expert. In still others it might require the immediate creation of an explicit therapeutic contract. Whatever tactic is adopted, the ultimate goal is to insure that the client faithfully carries out the directions or recommendations that are bound to follow.

The *analysis stage* involves a concentrated effort to focus on an area in which the patient is experiencing difficulty. Sometimes this task is relatively clear-cut, as in the case of a crisis, while at other times it is less obvious. Thus, in the case of a depression, the therapist might wish to explore why the onset has occurred at this particular time in the patient's life. It is in this stage that causal links are established and a tentative formulation arrived at. Delineating the problem to the satisfaction of both therapist and client marks the completion of the analysis stage.

The *planning stage,* as the name indicates, entails devising a treatment plan which will deal with the problem in as direct a manner as possible. Depending on the difficulty, the plan might involve a behavioral technique, suggestions for alternative interpersonal maneuvers, development of new relationships, role playing, and so on. Perhaps the critical variable in this phase is the client's active involvement in the decision-making process. The likelihood of the client engaging in new behavior is enhanced if he feels he has a say in what he will have to do.

The *implementation stage,* finally, sees the plan carried out. The crisis is resolved; the client tries out new ways of behaving; the symptom is eradicated or its significance reduced. The therapist is very active in this phase; rather than sitting back and simply observing, he directs, rewards, and provides feedback. If the plan does not seem to be working out, he suggests an alternative plan. In some instances, this stage may be followed by, or combined with, a recapitulation stage to firm up whatever new learning has occurred. Recapitulation, however, is often bypassed simply because new learning is thought to emerge directly out of successful resolution of the difficulty.

The model just described is not meant to be definitive. Rather, it is offered as a point of departure from which other brief psychotherapies could be conceptualized in process terms. Thus some, but not all, *short-term behavioristic* approaches might eliminate or de-emphasize the initial relationship stage. We might also expect *short-term analytic* approaches to include an "insight" stage, because of the psychoanalytic contention that new behavior without understanding lacks stability. As indicated earlier in this chapter, each unique system produces its own unique process.

The foregoing makes it obvious that one could construct the frameworks associated with different approaches to psychotherapy, be they extended or short-term, without too much difficulty. The major purpose of this book, however, is not to compile a compendium of stage frameworks—though this would be an intriguing task—but to provide a pragmatic interpersonal scheme for conducting psychotherapy. It is to this task that we now turn.

In the remaining chapters, the theoretical ideas that have been presented are applied to a therapy system focusing on interactional behavior. Using extensive case material, I will try to show how the process-rule scheme operates, first for individual and then for group psychotherapy. Since any therapy process derives from a unique model of human behavior, I will preface my efforts with a consideration of the model that underlies the interactional approach, addressing myself specifically to the ways people deal with one another in close interpersonal relationships.

SUMMARY

In the final analysis, the pressing and pervasive question, "What should I say (or do) when the patient says _____ ?" can best be answered by recourse to the stage account of the system within which one works. The rules contained within any single stage take into account the amount of movement made by the patient up to that point and dictate to a large extent the character of the therapist's response. This does not mean that the therapist is forced to ignore the unique needs of patients; on the contrary, rules better prepare him to address himself to these needs.

The stages of psychotherapy and their component rules represent a beginning attempt to clarify the therapist's task by indicating which techniques should be invoked in different phases of the treatment process. Observation of specific therapy transactions reveals that certain types of rules are predominately used in certain portions of the psychotherapy. In psychoanalysis, as we saw, interpretation is introduced rarely, if ever, in the initial phase of treatment. Nevertheless, psychoanalysis contains a fair number of interpretive rules. Systematic desensitization, on the other hand, is largely depicted in directive rules. A knowledge of a system's stages and its rules thus offers a means of describing a particular therapy and also provides a device for generating that system's techniques.

The practice of psychotherapy, however, involves more than rote rule-following: its successful execution depends upon the therapist's ability to perform complex transformations on clinical data. Again, this is not a mystical proposition but the basis for most of our reactions to the world about us. It is another way of saying that all of us construe the world in a somewhat different manner, depending upon the model of human behavior to which we subscribe. Thus, even in brief psychotherapy, the therapist must apply analytic, behavioristic, or social learning principles to material obtained in the analysis stage. The therapist's model differs from the layman's in that it is expected to be more clearly articulated and to cover a broader range of behavior. To the extent that this expectation is met, construction of case formulations is simplified. These formulations, together with interpretive, reactive and directive rules, generate the technique which constitutes the practice of psychotherapy.

3
Theory of Interactional Change

The term "interactional" has been used in various ways over the years and has come to mean different things for different people. In its traditional sense, the term roughly depicts the various social circumstances in which people satisfy their personal and idiosyncratic needs, such as the need for self-actualization, for impulse expression, for cognitive closure, and so on. Within this perspective, the social context is viewed merely as the backdrop within which these individual needs are met.

More recently, however, the term has been used to refer specifically to approaches where the focus is on the social encounter as a researchable phenomenon in its own right, where ". . . the initial and strategic point of study is the interaction between individuals" (Blumer, 1969, p. 108). According to this perspective,

> . . . one must appreciate the absolutely essential role that interaction plays in normal human development. Human beings are characterized by their strivings for and dependence upon interaction with other human beings. Such interaction is an end in itself, and interactional deprivation leads to anguish, loneliness, and depression. Interaction defines and affirms the humanness of the self. (Lennard et al., 1971, p. 48)

In approaches ranging from *Games People Play* (Berne, 1964) to the

42

theoretical assumptions of symbolic interactionism (Goffman, 1971; Lindesmith and Strauss, 1968; Stone and Farberman, 1970), the emphasis in shifting from the *individual* per se to the maneuvers and strategies by which individuals structure their *relationships*.

Interactional psychotherapy attempts to deal with these maneuvers, particularly where they lead to breakdowns in interpersonal functioning. The emphasis within this approach is on the nature of the patient's current interactions, with specific attention devoted to the unique character of the therapist-patient relationship. Before addressing ourselves to what there is about this relationship that lends itself to therapeutic change, we must first consider more generally how people deal with one another.

FOUNDATIONS OF INTERPERSONAL BEHAVIOR: PnP

In an earlier chapter, we proposed that every system of psychotherapy, explicitly or implicitly, makes certain assumptions about the motivational forces underlying human behavior. Psychoanalysis is based on a picture of man in which unconscious sexual and aggressive motives are prominent. The client-centered approach sees man as being motivated by the "actualizing tendency." The basic motive in the interactional approach to psychotherapy, in contrast, is social in character. Abbreviated *PnP*, for *People need People,* this motive is based on the assumption that much of human behavior is guided by the need to form close, ongoing relationships.

Although the notion of an affiliative motive is not particularly new, motivation of this sort has typically been relegated to a secondary or subsidiary position; people need people for nurturance in their early years, to satisfy their sexual needs, to facilitate actualization, to help secure other "primary and secondary reinforcements," etc. In such cases, the need for affiliation is thought to develop out of the necessity for satisfying more primary needs. The priorities, however, are reversed in the interactional approach. Within interactional therapy, *PnP* is regarded as the basic motive; it constitutes the guiding force that underlies the greater proportion of human behavior.

Classifying PnP in this way, as an assumption about man, obviates the need to further justify it. But since we will later have occasion to derive a number of important hypotheses from this assumption, we will briefly address ourselves to the question: What do people need people for? People need people for three basic reasons: to maintain the social roles they play, to facilitate cognitive functioning, and to provide emotional support. Each of these, alone or in combination, provides sufficient rationale for the strong vein of interdependency that characterizes human interaction.

Role Competency

The many ways in which people tend to work, play, and become intimate with one another are largely contained in the different social roles they assume. If we consider the various roles that one person plays in even a single day (worker, parent, spouse, etc.), we can see that every role requires a vastly different set of skills. Moreover, each requires a certain level of proficiency to be enacted with some degree of success.

Due to the complexity of social interaction, most people do not excel in all the roles they play. Some persons are good workers but are inept in family roles; some women make exciting lovers but leave a lot to be desired as housewives or mothers. People, however, are able to accept the fact that they may be mediocre or incompetent in some spheres of human functioning if they feel successful in others. Every individual, as a result, tries at the very least to excel in one of the roles he plays.

Success or competency in even one role, however, is not always easy to achieve. Role competency is a complex affair and is determined by a number of different factors. One must not only consider the proficiency of the person enacting the role but also the response of those who function as role complementors. Thus while the competency of a husband is tied to certain culturally linked "husbandlike" behaviors, it is also intimately related to the satisfaction of his wife. In a similar vein, the ultimate measure of a good administrator or a good teacher is inextricably tied to the respective performances of subordinates and students. The concept of competency, accordingly, cannot be meaningfully considered outside of a social context (Blumer, 1969).

Since role competency is determined in part by those who are the role complementors, "people need people" to help them adequately execute their roles. If all the world is a stage, people need people to validate their performances as successful actors. It is this consideration which leads to the inclusion of "role competency" as an essential ingredient of PnP.

Intellectual Validation

The ways in which human beings function to define and maintain reality for one another is a somewhat neglected topic in psychology. Although most theories of psychopathology suggest that a sense of reality is a prerequisite for adaptive functioning and that this "sense" is established very early in life, such theories say very little about the ways in which reality is *maintained.* A notable exception occurs in the work of Cameron and Magaret (1951). By inquiring into the ways in which people maintain some semblance of consistency in an ambiguous and often confusing world, they demonstrate how the social community continually acts to consensually validate the judgments and perceptions of its members. This crucial validation process may be denied an individual, however, if his sources of social contact are withdrawn. The result is the development of idiosyncratic systems of thought labeled *pseudo* and *autistic* "communities" which manifest themselves in delusional and hallucinatory phenomena.

The assumption that psychopathology derives largely from interpersonal isolation receives support from a number of different sources. One of the most revealing of these was an attempt to understand the "brainwashing" of American POWs during the Korean War. In a series of experiments conducted at McGill University, Heron and his associates (1961) demonstrated that short periods of isolation could lead to rather disturbing emotional and cognitive anomalies. Persons subjected to such conditions not only performed poorly on simple intellectual tasks but also experienced hallucinations. Findings of this sort coupled with animal work on the effect of isolation (e.g., Harlow et al., 1971) suggest that psychopathology may derive more from subtle patterns of alienation than previously thought.

One need not resort to dramatic findings such as these to verify the role that interpersonal feedback plays in stabilizing cognitive functions. A cursory examination of our everyday interactions yields numerous examples of this phenomenon. Thus the supposedly innocent remarks, "Do you think it's going to rain?" and "That was a tough exam!" not only fulfill social functions but also serve to corroborate private judgments regarding the state of the world. Most persons usually have answered such questions to their own satisfaction before conducting their inquiries. What they subtly ask of others is whether the others concur.

A great deal of our lives is spent making preliminary estimates about whether certain events will or will not occur and making judgments about how those around us are apt to behave. And most of us occasionally make mistakes. Some mistakes, particularly those concerning other people, can prove very costly—especially when they occur time and time again (Cashdan, 1966, p. 207). Wrongly estimating that it will rain may not bring much grief, but continually judging manipulative people as trustworthy, and vice versa, surely will. Using the social community as a source of interpersonal feedback helps minimize the confusion and anxiety to which errors of this sort lead. The phrase "intellectual validation" thus refers to the different ways in which people use others to monitor their judgmental skills.

Emotional Support

Misery, as the saying goes, loves company. So does joy. An examination of the different emotional responses that people experience, both positive and negative, testifies to their interpersonal character. Feelings of pleasure, annoyance, anger, and joy, while interpretable as "in-the-person" phenomena, are eminently more comprehensible when viewed interpersonally. Nevertheless, until very recently emotional experiences were construed primarily as intrapsychic events. The focus was on the feeling itself (sex, frustration, anger, etc.) with relatively little attention given to *who* was responsible for precipitating it.

The practice of construing emotional events as intrapsychic rather than interpersonal events can probably be traced to the development of psychoanalysis. Most emotional reactions, according to analytic doctrine, derive from the operation of the pleasure principle. The discharge of sexual and aggressive impulses leads to organismic gratification, while their damming up leads to tension. This tension, if unrelieved, leads to psychiatric disturbance. The emotional experiences that people have are thought to originate in physical, tissue-centered reactions having little direct relationship to the social environment.

From a social vantage point, emotional responses are interpreted as interpersonal phenomena. Whatever emotional reaction a person experiences is construed primarily in terms of the behavior of others. Rabkin (1970), in his book *Inner and Outer Space,* sums up this point of view with the statement, "... affect [is] a property of a social system. ...'Having' an emotion is not a subcutaneous fact; it is a type of transaction" (p. 63-65). People consequently get anxious not because they cannot express some inner tension, but because other people disappoint them, misuse them, or are insensitive to their needs. People experience "feelings of rejection" and "feelings of loneliness" because others withdraw from them or do not provide them with the attention and interpersonal respect they feel they deserve. Emotional support thus provides the third major reason for people needing people.

The assumption of PnP, in sum, is comprised of three crucial human requirements: the need to develop competency in the social roles one plays, the need for verifying one's perceptions and judgements, and the need for emotional sustenance. Each of these was briefly described to provide some picture of the ways people depend on others to maintain their social existence.

Granted that people need people, how do they "get" them? And assuming that they are successful in this regard, how do they "keep" them? The answers to these questions are not simple. They involve complex interpersonal concepts such as commitment, vulnerability, and intimacy, concepts that underlie the development of meaningful dyadic relationships. To gain an appreciation of how PnP is achieved, we therefore turn to a consideration of the ways in which people go about forming close, lasting, and mutually profitable relationships.

FORMATION OF DYADIC BONDS

The growth of a relationship is an intricate but nonetheless patterned process. Beginning with a series of hesitant, often clumsy forays, it moves with due deliberateness to the point where both participants respond to one another with confidence and trust. A prototype of this process is seen in the interplay between a young child and his puppy. The initial contact of the two almost always is marked by cautious, jerky movements. The child places his hand over the dog's head to pet him; the puppy quickly looks up; the child pulls away; and so on. The process is repeated in a stereotyped manner until a certain point is reached, after which subsequent moves are signaled by trust and affection. The two are then able to respond to one another spontaneously without the slightest hint of apprehension.

Formation of relationships in human beings is admittedly more complex, although the process bears strong structural similarities to the one just described. Strangers typically initiate contact through brief, hesitant forays. Such encounters, as we will show later, form the setting for subtle and safe information exchanges. Once a relationship progresses beyond this point, a series of intimate exchanges, characterized by risk and vulnerability, often follows. If all goes well, the stage is then set for greater involvement, whose onset is marked by behavioral reciprocity patterns and a mutual feeling of commitment. Obviously, things may go wrong at any point in the sequence, causing the relationship to either level off at an acquaintanceship level—or simply terminate.

Examining this process in more detail, we find that the initial phase in the development of a lasting relationship involves a series of subtle exploratory maneuvers aimed at gathering significant data about the other individual. Just as professional thieves case strange apartments before breaking in, so people case each other before making any unnecessary moves they may later regret. Interpersonal *casing* very often takes the form of exploratory maneuvers referred to as "small talk." Thus we typically hear new acquaintances ask questions or make remarks in the nature of "Where did you grow up?" "What does your father do?" "I love Bach," "X-rated movies should be banned!" The information contained in "small talk," however, is not trivial or insignificant. It contains data on a person's socioeconomic status, family background, intellectual tastes and emotional predispositions.

Perhaps the most salient feature of "small talk" is that it allows people to share a great deal of personal information while minimizing the interpersonal risk involved. One can, after all, disagree with another person's taste regarding an "X-rated" film without directly challenging his moral values. One can similarly gauge a person's cultural and socioeconomic level from another's father's occupation without having to directly inquire as to the family's stock holdings. While there are more direct ways to get such information, most are fraught with risk. Small talk consequently allows for the gathering of important information in as safe a manner as possible.

If casing operations uncover data that shed serious doubt on the dyad's future, the participants will usually attempt to "cool out" each other in as painless a manner as possible. Often this involves the use of face-saving rituals. The oft-used "I'm sorry but I'm busy that night" is one example of such a ritual, as is the prophetic "Don't call me, I'll call you." Although "cooling out" tactics are transparent, they appear to be preferable to the devastating self-doubts that typically accompany outright rejections (Goffman, 1968).

Assuming, however, that mutual exploration leaves both members of a dyad relatively satisfied, the relationship will likely progress into the next phase of the relationship process. In this middle phase, labeled *risky revealing,* the participants continue to trade personal information until one member finally divulges some fact or wish which places him in a highly vulnerable position. An adolescent confesses that his tales regarding the times he has "scored" are nothing more than wishful fantasies. A girl admits to strong sexual urges which she fears are signs of abnormality. One member in the dyad tells the other about periods of depression which have occasionally led to thoughts of suicide. By revealing a highly sensitive bit of personal information that could prove extremely damaging if made public, one member of the dyad concretely signifies his willingness to trust the other.

This heralds an important turning point in the relationship. The response of the member who is the recipient of the risky revelation now dictates whether or not the relationship will continue to grow. Of the many types of responses that might occur, one possibility is: "Don't worry; I'll keep it confidential." Another is: "You can tell me more if you like." Although both responses appear to be supportive, they leave the revealer in a vulnerable and disadvantaged position. The only response which will further the growth of the relationship is a reciprocal act of self-disclosure. Any other response, no matter how well intended, leads either to the dissolution of the relationship or to a low-level "let's be friends" arrangement.

The nonverbal counterpart of risky revealing is described by Watzlawick et al. in *Pragmatics of Human Communication* (1967). In their book, they relate the following tale of trust establishment between humans and bottle-nosed porpoises:

> The animals had obviously concluded that the hand is one of the most important and vulnerable parts of the human body. Each would seek to establish contact with a stranger by taking the human's hand into his mouth and gently squeezing it between his

jaws, which have sharp teeth and are powerful enough to bite the hand off cleanly. If the human would submit to this, the dolphin seemed to accept it as a message of complete trust. His next move was to reciprocate by placing the forward ventral portion of his body (*his* most vulnerable part, roughly equivalent in location to the human throat) upon the human's hand, leg, or foot, thereby signaling his trust in the friendly intentions of the human. This procedure, is, however, obviously fraught with possible misinterpretations at every step. (p. 104)

As is apparent, the process of trust establishment is a delicate touch-and-go affair, highly dependent on reciprocity for its success. The formation of a close, trusting relationship usually depends upon revealing *countered by* revealing and vulnerability *matched by* vulnerability.

While the self-exposure association with risky revealing plays a crucial part in the establishment of a close relationship, it is not the sine qua non in its maintenance. There are, after all, just so many things that two individuals can reveal to each other. The future of any relationship is embedded in the stylized behavioral patterns through which interpersonal transactions are structured. Labeled *strategies,* they dominate the final phase of relationship development.

STRATEGIES IN HUMAN RELATIONS

The term "strategy" as traditionally conceived of in the area of psychotherapy usually refers to certain tactical maneuvers on the part of *the therapist.* Used in this way, the term bears some similarity to the concept of a "rule." A strategy, however, may also be used to describe certain behaviors of *the client,* and it is in this sense that it is used in the following pages. Very briefly, a strategy will refer to relatively discrete modes of behavior through which individuals develop and maintain ongoing relations—with specific emphasis on those which are close and long-term. In other words, strategies are behavioral and communicative maneuvers that people use to fulfill PnP.

The concept of a strategy derives from a consideration of human interactions as exchanges. Within this framework, the ways in which individuals relate to one another are analyzed in terms of the gains and costs involved. Homans, one of the pioneering workers in this area, speaks of relationships as arrangements involving profit and loss (1958; 1961). Thibaut and Kelley, in their influential book *The Social Psychology of Groups* (1959), extend this analysis to a variety of interactions to help them predict the circumstances under which persons will continue to maintain dyadic relationships. They write:

> ... whatever the gratification achieved in dyads, however lofty or fine the motives satisfied may be, the relationship may be viewed as a trading or bargaining one. The basic assumption running throughout our analysis is that every individual voluntarily enters and stays in any relationship only as long as it is adequately satisfactory in terms of his rewards and costs. (p. 37)

Much of the social-psychological research on cooperation and conflict is based on this assumption (see Nemeth, 1972).

Entering the realm of personality and abnormal behavior, Carson (1969) has combined the exchange notions of Thibaut and Kelley with the interpersonal psychology of Leary (1957) and the interpersonal psychiatry of Sullivan (1953) to produce a stimulating analysis of the ways human beings manipulate each other to insure psychological survival. In his book, *Interaction Concepts of Personality,* Carson shows how people who have to deal with one another on an extended basis go about negotiating interpersonal "contracts" as a means of satisfying their personal demands. He demonstrates, moreover, how in some instances contracts may be deliberately violated so that one member of a dyad ends up chronically exploited. Such developments are synonymous with the emergence of "psychopathology."

Within Carson's framework, and that of Thibaut and Kelley's as well, a concept of paramount importance is that of an interpersonal bargain. In pure economic terms, a good bargain is one in which maximum possible return is obtained for minimum outlay. In interpersonal exchanges, a good bargain occurs when PnP is fulfilled without sacrificing too much in the way of personal comfort and self-esteem. Bad bargains see PnP achieved at the cost of much pain and humiliation.

Human relationships, unfortunately, contain an abundance of bad bargains. In much the same way that one can be short-changed in an economic transaction, one can also be cheated in a social transaction. Where two people negotiate for the use of each other, strategies function as interpersonal "chips," behavioral devices which are used to reduce the risk of being cheated. They represent each person's idiosyncratic attempt to maximize gain (fulfill PnP) and minimize cost (avoid pain and disappointment) in relationships where a long-term commitment is at stake.

Strategies may take many different forms, some of which are potentially more maladaptive than others. Sadism, promiscuity, and parasitism, for example, represent just a few of the ways in which people structure their relationships maladaptively. *Games People Play* (Berne, 1964) is essentially a compilation of interpersonal tactics and maneuvers that could easily fall under the rubric of "maladaptive strategies." Strictly speaking, however, a strategy's maladaptiveness is not a function of the strategy itself but of the way it meets or fails to meet the needs of the recipients. Sadism is not particularly maladaptive in the context of a sado-masochistic relationship; it becomes so when practiced on an unwilling partner. In a similar vein, sexuality is not maladaptive in the "showgirl-sugar daddy" arrangement. It is only when the implicit contractual agreements are violated—the show girl insisting on marriage, for example—that the strategy in question takes on a maladaptive flavor.

A close examination of the kinds of difficulties people experience in our society reveals that some strategies tend to lead to more difficulty than others. Among these, and perhaps the most visible, are sexuality, dependency, and martyr strategies. At least one of these is often implicated in cases involving psychological disturbance.

In the *sexuality strategy*, sex constitutes the unitary mode through which an individual conducts his interpersonal dealings. Whether we are speaking of subtle but chronic flirtatiousness or blatant promiscuity, it is the use of sex which forms as well as maintains close relationships. Within such relationships, sex is relied upon to settle personal disputes, relieve boredom, and maintain dominance-submission patterns. As such, it becomes *the* medium of social exchange rather than just one of many ways in which two people can conjointly satisfy their needs.

Sexual strategies are only pathological when they come to dominate long-term relationships; they are not particularly maladaptive as short-term solutions. During adolescence, for example, the search for intimacy, attention, and even respect leads many young people to occasionally use their bodies as bartering mediums. It is only when such patterns come to dominate one's extended relationships and persist into adulthood that we suspect that something is very wrong. The terms "Don Juan," "stud," and "easy make" reflect the contemptuous stance taken toward sexual strategists and provide us with some insight into the types of difficulties such persons are apt to encounter.

Dependency strategies take the form of helper-helpee arrangements in which one member of the dyad constantly solicits advice, direction, and assistance from the other. Within this particular pattern, the strategist hooks his target by convincing him that he (the strategist) would be unable to maintain himself without continual guidance and support. Although the strategist's request for assistance may appear on the surface to be straightforward and innocuous, it reflects the deeper and more devious message, "I can't live without you!" In extreme instances, this threat may be communicated by means of suicide attempts.

Satisfying persons who employ dependency strategies is a herculean task, and it is thus not surprising to find the targets of such strategies reacting with anger and resentment. Although at first the target may be led to believe that he will only be needed on rare occasions, he eventually finds that he is expected to always be "on call." Refusal to comply is complicated by the threat of suicide that hangs over his head. The resultant feelings of hostility and impotency that grow out of a realization that one is being used and cannot do anything about it makes relationships involving dependency strategies particularly stormy.

The *martyr strategy* bears a similarity to the dependency strategy in that it also emerges out of a helper-helpee arrangement. This time, however, the strategist adopts the role of *helper* and places his target in a helpee role. Adapting a self-effacing, self-sacrificial pose, martyr strategists devote themselves to convincing their targets that they (the target) could not possibly manage on their own. The techniques employed to achieve this goal include the subtle manipulation of guilt feelings as well as other maneuvers designed to create a sense of helplessness in the target. Whereas the implicit threat in the dependency strategy is, "I'll die without you," in the martyr strategy it is, *"You'll* die without me!"

Some insight into the operation of martyr strategies is offered by Dan Greenburg in *How to Be a Jewish Mother* (1964). In one section of his book, the author lists "Seven Basic Sacrifices" that a mother can make for her child:

(1) Stay up all night to prepare him a big breakfast.

(2) Go without lunch so you can put an extra apple in his lunchpail.

(3) Give up an evening of work with a charitable institution so that he can have the car on a date.

(4) Tolerate the girl he's dating.

(5) Don't let him know you fainted twice in the supermarket from fatigue. (But make sure he knows you're not letting him know.)

(6) When he comes home from the dentist, take over his toothache for him.

(7) Open his bedroom window wider so he can have more fresh air, and close your own so you don't use up the supply.

Although presented in tongue-in-cheek fashion, each "sacrifice" obviously contains more than a grain of truth. The author, moreover, points out that one doesn't have to be Jewish to be a Jewish mother. It is perhaps just as obvious that one doesn't have to be a mother.

The sexuality, dependency, and martyr strategies provide three common examples of maladaptive strategies. Each represents a set of exploitive behavioral maneuvers used to structure long-term personal relationships. Together, they depict the turns that interpersonal relations can take when people are unwilling or unable to take the risks inherent in human relationships.

Before leaving the topic of maladaptive strategies, we should reiterate that it is not the content of a strategy that determines its maladaptiveness but rather the lack of reciprocity in the dyad. Some of the strategies that were described can take on adaptive qualities if the participants are willing to acknowledge and meet the demands that each strategy implicitly places on the other. This is often not the case, and the result is a series of pathological and destructive interactions. Maladaptive strategies, in short, are marked by exploitive demands and a one-dimensional manner of structuring one's interpersonal dealings.

Considering all that has been said, what is the nature of adaptive relating? How do people structure their ongoing relationships so as to facilitate interpersonal growth? The answer is embedded in behavioral patterns marked by risk and reciprocity, patterns which fall under the heading of *selfish altruism*.

The term "altruism" as it is typically used denotes a regard for and devotion to the interests of others. Altruism, as such, tends to fall into the category of a trait, i.e., an enduring personality characteristic. Combined with the word "selfish," it seems patently out of place. Altruism, however, need not be considered a characteristic or trait; it can be viewed as a *means* through which people achieve their interpersonal goals. In our case, that goal is satisfaction of PnP.

In the framework we are developing, selfish altruism represents *the* adaptive strategy. It is the generic label for a wide variety of behaviors in which ostensibly selfless actions are engaged in for purposes of satisfying long-term needs. The selfish altruist, accordingly, is the person who is concerned first and foremost with providing emotional support for his counterpart in a relationship and in meeting his partner's role requirements. In a marital interaction, for example, such a person is concerned first with making his partner a competent husband or wife—a complex endeavor involving sexual support, maintenance of social appearances, help with in-laws, etc. His own personal needs, at least temporarily, are relegated to a secondary position.

The concept of selfish altruism deviates somewhat from other views of interpersonal reciprocity. Jackson's (1965) *quid pro quo* (literally "something for something") suggests that reciprocity is maintained through a rather concrete tit-for-tat arrangement. According to the quid pro quo, people stay in a relationship because of the rewards derived from continued emotional back-scratching. Gouldner (1960) suggests that close relationships are maintained through a process of social indeterminancy. Participants in close interactions, he contends, maintain their relationships because they are ignorant of the precise exchange parameters; they are thus unable to tell whether or not they are being cheated.

Selfish altruism, in contrast, is not contingent on immediate reinforcement, nor is it based on vague and ill-defined expectations. Like other strategies, it represents a series of relatively long-term behavioral maneuvers designed to insure the perpetuation of a mutually gratifying relationship. Unlike other strategies, however, it involves a relatively long period of self-denial as a means of insuring future gratification.

Adopting selfish altruism as one's interpersonal *modus operandi* is admittedly a risky proposition. One can invest an enormous amount of intellectual and emotional energy in another human being and come up short-changed or even empty-handed. Despite this, selfish altruism probably has the best chance of succeeding among the various dyadic arrangements that are available. While personal needs are temporarily sacrificed in this strategy, they nonetheless stand the best chance of being met in the long run. Most other dyadic arrangements typically involve conditional commitments and counter-commitments and frequently lead to the development of mistrust and apprehension.

Although selfish altruism can fail—as can any strategy—the probability of its succeeding can be greatly enhanced if it is preceded by risky revealing. Persons who successfully risk self-exposure and thereby develop a modicum of trust in each other are in a much better position to take relatively extended "altruistic" risks. Successful relationships when historically retraced, therefore, reveal sequential contact operations involving risky revealing followed by selfish altruism. Unsuccessful relationships either show little evidence of risky revealing, or, if it has taken place, no attempt to follow it up with altruistic maneuvers. It is within relationships such as these that maladaptive strategies tend to be most prominently displayed.

STRATEGIES, SYMPTOMS, AND PSYCHIATRY

The emphasis in this chapter has until now been placed on the strategies that people use to deal with one another. Some of these strategies are highly exploitive and maladaptive, and lead to severe problems in maintaining productive relationships. Our discussion of these strategies, however, has not revolved around the usual psychiatric foci, i.e., symptoms. It would thus seem instructive to delve briefly into the realm of psychiatry to demonstrate how psychiatric symptoms are construed in strategic terms.

An examination of the various psychiatric syndromes reveals that each entails diminished interpersonal regard, rejection, or interpersonal loss—in short, failure to strategically satisfy PnP. Differences among syndromes, however, lie less in the strategies employed (strategies cut across syndromes) than in unique deficits in the components of PnP. Each syndrome represents to a varying extent the patient's inability to achieve role competency, intellectual validation, emotional support, or some combination thereof.

The specific symptoms that comprise the psychiatric syndromes, regardless of the form they take, represent attempts to rescue or reinstitute foundering relationships. Sexual symptoms (impotence and frigidity, for example), depression, and even delusions are telling indications of a strategy's failure to bind a relationship; the main difference between neurotic and psychotic symptoms is that in the latter, efforts to satisfy PnP have largely been abandoned. The functional similarity among psychiatric symptoms is depicted in the following case study involving a "psychotic" depression preceded by "neurotic" symptomatology.

The patient, a plain-looking woman in her early thirties, was seen in a rural community mental health center. The wife of a moderately successful farmer, she was referred to the clinic by her family physician because of difficulty in swallowing and progressive loss of interest in her daily activities. Although a preliminary diagnosis of Globbus Pallidus (an hysterical disorder thought to derive from fears and fantasies regarding fellatio) was offered by the clinic psychiatrist, an intensive interview revealed that the patient and her husband led a highly conventional and satisfactory sex life.

A brief social history revealed that the patient had been married for three years and had one small child. She and her husband lived a simple but nevertheless satisfying existence and took a lot of pride in the life they had built together. The husband worked hard making the farm successful while the wife did the sort of things that the wives of farmers in this area usually did; she sewed, tended a vegetable garden, and took care of the few farm animals they owned.

A detailed examination of the patient's interactions revealed that she was a somewhat dependent woman; this, however, did not lead to any particular problem in the marital relationship. The husband was always available to help or advise his wife and seemed perfectly content to do so. Evenings were spent together conversing, watching TV, and listening to music. The patient had taken piano lessons prior to her marriage and for a wedding gift was given a piano by her husband. She took great pride in her playing and only while discussing her musical interests did she become animated. In most of the interview, though, she gave the impression of being disinterested and resigned.

The patient's difficulty in swallowing began approximately

three weeks prior to her referral; between that time and the time she arrived at the clinic, her condition had progressively worsened. The onset of the symptom was roughly correlated with a visit by her mother-in-law, a visit that not only was unexpected but was of indeterminate length. The mother-in-law simply arrived one day, announced that she was going to stay "for a while," and casually settled in. The son "jokingly" allayed his wife's concerns by insisting that his mother would probably leave "as soon as she gets tired of us."

The mother's sudden entry into the household marked the beginning of a subtle but nonetheless significant change in the wife's position vis à vis the husband. From the moment the mother arrived, she dominated her son's time, in effect relegating the husband-wife relationship to a subordinate status. She overindulged her son, began to "correct" many of the patient's housework patterns (cleaning, cooking, etc.), and continually irritated the patient by endlessly commenting on what a wonderful, hardworking husband her son was.

The patient, unfortunately, found it impossible to discuss her predicament directly with her husband. Because of what she correctly perceived as an intense bond between mother and son, she felt that any complaint would be construed as an attack on the mother. Her one mild complaint led to the husband's response of, "Mother doesn't mean any harm; she loves us both and just wants to be with us." The straw that broke the camel's back, however, occurred one evening when the mother asked the patient if she would mind not playing the piano during her visit since it gave her a headache. The patient's symptom developed soon afterwards.

In the first few clinic visits, the patient was encouraged to resume her normal activities. (Since the mother arrived, the patient had almost totally relinquished her household responsibilities.) An effort was also made to get her to discuss whatever feelings of anger or frustration she might have; she declined, however, insisting that she bore no animosity toward either her mother-in-law or her husband. Eventually, though, the patient started to vent her annoyance toward the mother-in-law. As the sessions progressed, she was also able to pinpoint the specific circumstances under which her inability to swallow worsened.

Not surprisingly, the condition was exacerbated whenever all three family members were together.

In one therapy session, the patient spent a considerable portion of time describing the various indignities heaped upon her. Toward the end of the session, I "casually" remarked, "Sound's like your mother-in-law is pretty hard to swallow." The patient rose from her chair, gave me a cold, hard stare, and left without saying a word. She returned next week reporting that her symptom had practically disappeared; she complained, however, of listlessness and a bad case of "the blues." Soon afterwards she had to be hospitalized for severe depression.

Because the mental hospital to which the patient was sent was over fifty miles from her home, a single visit by the husband took up to three hours (two hours spent traveling back and forth and one hour actually spent in visiting). Visiting times at the hospital were fairly flexible and visiting was encouraged so that the husband also often spent entire weekends with his wife. These time-consuming excursions, added to the time he spent in the fields, left him little time to devote to his mother. As a result, she packed her bags, terminated her visit, and returned to her own home. The patient's depression dissipated within a few weeks, after which she returned to the farm and resumed a normal existence.

The preceding case study obviously was not offered as an example of refined therapeutic technique. The interpretation was undoubtably ill-timed; if anything, it functioned to prematurely rob the patient of an important communicative outlet. Nevertheless, the case is instructive in that it vividly portrays the ways in which symptoms bespeak social concerns and are interpersonally restitutive in character.

Even in disturbances as severe as schizophrenia (the avoidance strategy, par excellence), a residual effort remains to maintain some thread of a relationship. Rokeach (1964), in his extensive study of three paranoid schizophrenics *The Three Christs of Ypsilanti*, writes, "In the course of our study we learned ... that psychosis is a far cry from the happy state that some make it out to be; that it may sometimes represent the best terms a person can come to with life; that psychotics, having good reason to flee human companionship, nevertheless crave it" (p. 331).

Whether we are speaking of schizophrenic symptoms, an inability to swallow, or chronic depression, psychiatric symptoms allow the patient to comment on his current interpersonal plight without risking open and dangerous confrontation. Accordingly, the different psychiatric syndromes underscore the inability of certain human beings to successfully meet the personal demands symbolized by PnP. Neuroses represent maladaptive strategies frozen in perseverative, unproductive patterns, while psychoses signify the end result of conditioned strategic failures. Taken together, the psychiatric syndromes depict some of the more pathological solutions people adopt in trying to deal with unproductive relationships.

IMPLICATIONS FOR CHANGE

It is apparent by now that the concept of a strategy will play an important role in planning therapeutic change. Regardless of the nature of the presenting problem, the ultimate goal in the interactional approach will involve modifying maladaptive strategies. The entire therapeutic procedure is geared towards undermining such strategies and substituting behavioral strategies which have a greater potential for success.

Successful enactment of strategic change, however, is not a simple matter. Since any strategy, maladaptive or otherwise, constitutes an individual's longstanding techniques for structuring close relationships, it is highly resistant to change. Maladaptive strategies are particularly impervious since they often signify last-ditch attempts to preserve some semblance of stability in the patient's life. Any effort to alter them will understandably be fought tooth and nail.

Bearing this in mind, how does one go about modifying maladaptive strategies? One possibility is to help the patient gain insight into why he behaves in self-defeating ways. However, this frequently fails. People do not change their strategies simply because they come to better understand why they behave the way they do. People do respond, on the other hand, to strategic failures and successes. Since strategies persist primarily because of their implicit payoffs, it seems logical to expect that manipulating the payoffs might result in meaningful change.

Of the many relationships in the client's life that have significant payoffs, the one to which the therapist has most immediate access involves himself. The fact that the patient comes to the therapist for help, de facto, imbues him with a certain amount of utility. By capitalizing on this often neglected but highly significant fact, the therapist is able to foster the development of maladaptive strategies within the therapy itself. He is then in a position to deal with the client's "pathology" directly, through the medium of the client-therapist relationship. The way in which this is accomplished constitutes the subject of the next chapter.

We may conclude and briefly summarize this chapter by stating that for reasons revolving about the maintenance of personal integrity (PnP), people develop relatively discrete interpersonal patterns (strategies) to structure their intimate relationships. When these strategies take on a lopsided, exploitive character, they are considered maladaptive, which is to say that they may result in dyadic breakdowns and psychiatric disturbance. Interactional psychotherapy attempts to modify these strategies by manipulating payoffs in the patient's ongoing relationships, the most immediate of which involves his relationship with the therapist.

4
Interactional Individual Therapy

Interactional psychotherapy is a treatment process that deals with maladaptive strategies as they present themselves in the course of treatment. The goal of treatment is to guide the client through a series of sequential learning experiences in order to replace maladaptive patterns with more productive ways of relating. A synopsis of the therapy process begins with the therapist establishing a relationship in which he takes on the characteristics of "a significant figure," one capable of potentially satisfying PnP. Once this happens, maladaptive strategies emerge spontaneously as the client attempts to bind the therapist in an intimate and extended relationship. The therapist thereafter manipulates ensuing exchanges so that the client is forced to relinquish his strategy if he is to maintain the relationship. The conclusion of therapy is marked by the emergence of new ways of relating, reflected in more mature and adaptive client-therapist exchanges.

The interactional psychotherapy process is comprised of five relatively discrete stages. They are:

Stage One: Hooking
Stage Two: Maladaptive Strategies
Stage Three: Stripping

Stage Four: Adaptive Strategies
Stage Five: Unhooking (Termination)

Each stage involves certain therapist techniques as well as some sort of incremental change on the part of the client.

In the following pages, an attempt will be made to describe in as precise terms as possible the stage-related movement of both client and therapist, movement which, when viewed longitudinally, constitutes the therapy process. In each stage, examples distilled from a number of psychotherapies are presented as illustrations. In addition, a single case study is followed from its inception to its completion. The case in point concerns that of a young woman named Beth who was self-referred to a psychotherapy clinic.

Beth, age twenty-six, single, and fairly attractive, was seeking therapy for the first time. On leave of absence from her job as a junior buyer for a large department store, she was spending the summer attending a midwestern university summer school to complete her Master's degree in Marketing. Her application to the psychotherapy clinic was prompted by what was vaguely described as "anxiety over schoolwork."

The initial interview was spent gathering background data, trying to determine how debilitating her anxiety was, and pinpointing the circumstances under which it occurred. After much hedging, the client revealed that she had "slightly" misrepresented her position; she was indeed anxious, but not over schoolwork. Instead she was deeply apprehensive over a possible resumption of an earlier homosexual relationship which had been terminated upon her return to school; more generally she was concerned about the possibility that she might fall into a chronic homosexual lifestyle.

The relationship involved a lengthy affair with an older woman who was a senior buyer in the department store where Beth had been employed. The affair lasted over a period of seven months, at the end of which the two were seeing each other three or four evenings a week. The affair was terminated with much bitterness on Beth's part by the older woman, who insisted that discovery of their relationship was imminent and would ruin both of their careers.

The initial interview revealed some of the strong doubts Beth had about herself and accentuated her ambivalence about the type of lifestyle she wanted to lead. Although she would be returning to work in another department, she felt that she might impulsively try to resume her relationship with her ex-partner. She was thus torn between homosexual impulses and the desire to lead a "straight" life.

An inquiry into the client's past revealed more than the usual amount of parental psychopathology. The father was a rather weak, ineffectual person who nonetheless formed the emotional focus for the client's early childhood. A chronic alcoholic, he occasionally made sexual advances toward Beth but in his lucid moments radiated concern over her welfare. Her mother was portrayed as a rather distant figure with a history of repeated hospitalization for schizophrenia. At the time the client entered therapy, her parents were divorced; the father, a professional man, remained in their hometown, while the mother moved to Atlanta where she ran a small but successful interior decorating business.

The client's very early years were spent in this rather disruptive household, although most of her school years after the age of nine were spent in a Catholic boarding school. While there, she became closely attached to one of the young nuns. Their relationship was described as "mainly platonic," although Beth admitted being sexually aroused on occasions when her older companion stroked her back.

During her college years, Beth occasionally dated boys but always felt uncomfortable in their presence. She tended to be promiscuous and found on repeated occasions that she was unable to form a lasting relationship. After graduation, she took a position as a junior buyer at a well-known department store; there she met the older woman and the two started going to plays and dinner together. Beth's existence was a lonely one and she welcomed the activities that the two shared. Eventually the older woman "seduced" her, a feat accomplished with little resistance on Beth's part, and the two began seeing each other regularly. From Beth's description, however, the relationship seemed more distinctive for its mother-daughter overtones than for its sexual features. The relationship, in any event, lasted only seven months, and at the time Beth entered treatment she was not actively involved with anyone.

Subsequent developments in the case are described in the context of specific stages. We therefore turn to the process itself and to the first stage of treatment.

STAGE ONE: HOOKING

The term *hooking* refers to a process in which the therapist is transformed from a relatively distant and removed professional figure into someone who is perceived as warm, caring and involved—in short, into what is referred to as "a significant figure." The purpose of this transformation is twofold. The most immediate purpose is to set the stage for the emergence of the client's maladaptive strategy. Such strategies, although occasionally manifested in superficial relationships, are depicted most saliently in relationships characterized by intimacy and commitment. In order for the strategy to fully emerge in subsequent stages, therefore, the therapist must be perceived as a significant figure—a person who in the client's eyes can potentially satisfy PnP.

The second reason for hooking is to provide the client with a motive for remaining in therapy later, when the going gets rough. The question of what actually keeps the client in therapy is usually not at issue early in the treatment process; anxious and symptomatic, he is hurting and is willing to undergo whatever is necessary to secure relief. Later in treatment, however, matters are not this simple. The urgency and intensity of the client's complaints have often diminished, perhaps even disappeared, but still he continues to be exposed to a great deal of stress in therapy. Faced with disquieting insights and painful confrontations, there often arises a temptation to bolt, which, if acted upon, could lead to premature termination. Hooking anticipates this problem by creating a client-therapist relationship to fill the motivational void. The client remains in treatment not because of great psychological pain, not because of esoteric notions involving personal growth, but because he has become very invested in the therapist.

Generally speaking, hooking is accomplished by the implementation of two rules: *emotional coupling* and *advising*. Each in its own way is designed to capitalize on the nature of the helping relationship and thus set the stage for later developments in the treatment process.

Together they generate the concrete responses that act to bind the client to the therapist.

Emotional Coupling

One of the ways in which the therapist becomes " a significant figure" is by convincing the client that his thoughts and feelings are accurately and sympathetically perceived. Emotional coupling refers to a wide variety of techniques designed to persuade the client that the therapist is able to appreciate and share his deepest feelings. With roots in the client-centered approach to treatment, emotional coupling is basically the communication of empathic understanding. When used judiciously, it acts to persuade the client that he and the therapist are on the same emotional wavelength.

Emotional coupling can be construed as a two-part process. The first part entails making a best guess as to the emotional component of the client's factual statements; the second involves communicating ("mirroring") this to him. In most instances, the process is fairly straightforward, as seen in examples taken from two different patients:

> *Cl:*   I break out into a cold sweat every time he touches me.
> *Th:*   Physical contact makes you terribly *uncomfortable.*

or,

> *Cl:*   I'm sure they [other ward patients] are poisoning my food.
> *Th:*   It makes you *nervous* about whom you can trust.

In both these examples, the therapist takes what is essentially a factual report, extracts what appears to be the emotional reaction associated with it, and mirrors it for the client.

Application of the emotional coupling rule leads to a variety of statements that take the form of:

"It makes you *happy* when you talk about _____."

"You seem *upset* whenever the subject of _____ comes up."

"You're really *annoyed* at _____."

"_____ makes you *embarrassed.*"

Such comments function to persuade the client that the therapist is capable of appreciating what he really is experiencing.

The therapist's ability to correctly "guess" what the client feels is aided by several considerations. The first is the assumption that most statements are made up of affective as well as factual components; one can thus feel relatively confident in assuming that the client feels something about what he is relating even if he does not openly reveal it. Another factor is that many of the client's statements tend to be accompanied by nonverbal indicators such as rapid breathing, blushing, teariness, and intonation (e.g., sarcasm), which are fairly reliable "giveaways" as to the nature of his emotional response. Finally, a great many affectively tinged statements contain emotional dualities: the mention of hate frequently implies the presence of love; dominance, submission; aloofness, warmth; and so on. The therapist accordingly is on fairly safe ground if he alludes to the presence of one whenever the other is being overemphasized.

This is demonstrated in the following excerpt in which a recently divorced young woman bitterly describes her ex-husband:

> *Cl:*   He used to ... drink ... *(Long pause)*
> *Th:*   ... and ...
> *Cl:*   ... the bum beat me ...
> *Th:*   ... and ...
> *Cl:*   ... he really didn't care about the family ...
> *Th:*   ... and you wish you had him back.

The client immediately began sobbing, after which she slowly started to talk about her loneliness and deep concern over bringing up her young son without a father.

It may on the surface seem risky to comment on love in the face of anger, on submission in the context of power, and so on. But generally speaking, little risk is actually involved. Ambivalent feelings play a significant role in much of man's affairs, so that one can feel reasonably secure in highlighting one emotional response when its antithesis is being emphasized. Whether the therapist takes risky guesses in regard to the client's feelings or simply mirrors emotions that are close to the surface, his behavior in any case tends to be guided by the emotional coupling rule.

Advising

In the present context, advising essentially refers to concrete suggestions for action tempered by regard for the stage's goal. Since the primary concern is hooking the client, the therapist must be careful not to offer advice that is likely to result in failure or in other ways compromise his position as a "significant" figure.

Perhaps the simplest and safest advising in which the therapist can engage occurs, paradoxically, where there is no decision at stake. In some instances, clients ask for help in making a "decision" when one has already been made. Students may ask for help in deciding whether they should leave school after they have decided to withdraw; clients ask whether they should leave their wives or husbands after they have already separated. What is actually being solicited in such instances is not advice but support. This the therapist can provide without undue difficulty or risk. Another type of "riskless advice-giving" concerns situations in which the client is faced with alternatives that are equally appealing so that he has difficulty making up his mind. Where there is an obvious approach-approach conflict, a gentle nudge can function to place the therapist in an advantageous light.

More often though, the advice that clients seek does bear on actual decisions involving positive and negative outcomes. It is here that the therapist must be especially careful. If he is to insure his status as a "significant figure" (the primary goal of Stage One), he must take care not to be maneuvered into offering advice that may play a part in the client's interpersonal fiascos. Most clients not only have a history of chronic social blunders but are also expert at distorting advice and externalizing blame. Thus there is more to be lost by offering advice than by tactfully declining, perhaps one of the major reasons that many therapists eschew advice-giving.*

Advice-giving, nonetheless, can be put to good use as a therapeutic technique if it is employed properly. The knack involves offering suggestions only when they have a high probability of success and to make sure that an "out" is available should they fail. The "out" entails subtly placing the responsibility for whatever action is taken squarely in the client's lap. Thus, advice such as:

---

* There obviously are other reasons for refusing advice. In psychoanalysis, for example, refusals of this type are specifically designed to increase frustration.

"Why don't you try to be a little more outspoken with your mother?"

should be more properly phrased:

"It seems to me that *you would like* to be a little more outspoken with your mother."

Although both statements can potentially satisfy the client's need to be more assertive, the second is less likely to result in the therapist being blamed if the client fails in his efforts.

This rule, when applied, leads to remarks that take the following form:

"It seems to me that *you want* to . . ."

"*You might* want to go ahead and act on *your* wish to . . ."

"If *you decide* that way, *you could* go ahead and . . ."

By placing the locus of responsibility in the client, the therapist avoids losing the client's confidence if the advice fails.

A rather straightforward example of advising occurred in the early stages of work with Beth:

In one of the early therapy sessions, Beth announced that prior to her entry into therapy, she had arranged a meeting with her mother in Washington, D. C. Beth was scheduled to attend a one-day marketing conference in the city and in a letter to her mother had casually mentioned this. Her mother wrote back suggesting they spend the day together and offered to fly to Washington to meet her. Although Beth had agreed to this arrangement, she now found herself becoming increasingly anxious about the impending meeting.

The two had agreed to meet in Beth's hotel room, where they felt they could talk to one another undisturbed. This arrangement in particular made Beth very nervous. Although it was not precisely clear what it was she feared (homosexual impulses towards her mother, acting out angry feelings, etc.), one thing was clear: Beth was terribly apprehensive about meeting her mother within the confines of a small room. I therefore suggested that the two meet at the Lincoln Memorial, and from there go to lunch together; afterwards they could visit the National Art

Gallery where they might talk at leisure while viewing the exhibits.

Beth followed my suggestion and returned to the next therapy session in a euphoric mood. The meeting had gone off without a hitch; the two spent a pleasant day together and even arranged a similar rendezvous a few months hence. Beth was delighted with the outcome.

It is obvious that Beth's distress could have conceivably provided a jumping-off point for an interpretive exploration of the mother-daughter relationship. Such a move in this stage of treatment would have been premature and potentially disastrous. Arguments regarding "flight into health" notwithstanding, many clients are scared off in the early parts of treatment simply because they are exposed to material they are not capable of assimilating. Premature terminations can be averted if the beginning therapist remembers that his goal in Stage One is not to interpret, confront, or in any other way effect miraculous cures, but merely to hook.

Successful completion of Stage One is achieved when the client reports feeling better, or at least indicates that he is relatively content with the course of treatment. The combination of emotional coupling and advising provides the client with the feeling that he has gained a knowledgeable, understanding, and accepting partner in his battle against the viscissitudes of life. Filled with a sense of accomplishment, he now looks forward to his sessions. Beth, for example, could not contain her appreciation after the meeting with her mother and attributed the success of the meeting to her progress in therapy. An appreciative mood now fills the air and the client regularly meets his appointments not because he is compelled to but because he wants to. This telltale shift in attitude marks the completion of Stage One and indicates that it is time to move on to the next stage.

STAGE TWO:
MALADAPTIVE STRATEGIES

The major behavioral phenomenon in Stage Two is the appearance of the client's maladaptive strategy. Acting on the assumption that the possibility for PnP gratification lies within the therapy itself, an assumption primed by the gratifying events of Stage One, the client makes a concerted effort to deepen the relationship. In Stage Two, the client's unique manner of dealing with people, *his* way of hooking others, starts to make its presence known.

Although the impetus behind PnP virtually guarantees the appearance of the client's strategy, strategic demands invariably appear at first in disguised form. Direct and concrete relational statements are hardly ever laid out on the table for the simple reason that they leave one highly vulnerable and open to direct and immediate rejection. Clients, therefore, are much more apt to phrase their problems in terms of the "there and then," focusing on relationships outside the therapy and on events occurring early in life, than to discuss what is going on in the "here and now."

The basic rule associated with Stage Two is designed to counter this tendency. Labeled the *immediacy rule,* it involves leading the client to the present whenever he is mired in the past and into the therapy room whenever he gravitates to events outside of it. Remembering that the therapist is trying to structure a treatment process revolving about the nature of the immediate relationship, we can appreciate the signal importance of this rule.

Application of the immediacy rule is meant to draw the client through the different communicative levels that make up therapeutic interaction. Among these it is possible to extract three, each varying on an immediacy dimension:

1. Talk of early experiences (focus on childhood friends, parental relations, etc.)
2. Talk of current relationships (focus on employer, spouse, boyfriend, etc.)
3. Talk about therapy relationship (focus on therapist)

By depicting levels on a dimension of interpersonal immediacy, the foregoing describes the communicational progression expected to occur in Stage Two. As such, it represents the stage's behavioral shift.

It is relatively simple to get from level one to two; many clients, in fact, start off at the second level. Those who chronically "regress" to level one, or who start there and cannot seem to progress, usually can be drawn to level two simply by posing leading questions and reorienting the conversation. It is a little more difficult to progress from level two to what is going on *in* the therapy. This nevertheless can be facilitated by the gradual introduction of comments such as:

Th: How do *you* feel about telling *me* _____ ?

Th: Last week *you* seemed to get angry when *I* said _____ .

Th: How do *you* think *I* react when you say _____ ?

Movement from level two to three can also be fostered by interpreting the client's "outside" remarks as direct comments on the therapy relationship. Thus when the client says:

"I felt like acting more aggressively towards my ·husband this past week,"

the therapist might reply:

"I think that perhaps you're saying you'd like to be able to be more aggressive in here."

Although the client at times may insist that he is being misread, the therapist should not give up too easily. He will not be too far off the mark if he assumes that many of the client's utterances actually reflect on the immediate interaction.

As the therapist progressively establishes the "here and now" framework of the therapy, most clients tend to become increasingly uneasy. This is understandable since the closer the therapist gets to the strategy, the greater the risk of rejection becomes. The client often responds to the perceived threat by playing "what-if" games. In the hope of anticipating how the therapist might respond if he (the client) actually committed himself, the client starts structuring the relationship in conditional terms. As Stage Two progresses, the interaction is increasingly marked by statements on the client's part that take the form of:

"I wonder what *you'd* say *if* . . . ?"

and

"I wonder what *you'd* do *if* . . . ?"

Conditional inquiries such as these reflect the client's concern with the therapist's feelings while simultaneously reiterating his unwillingness to risk himself.

If the therapist wishes to deal effectively with the client's strategy, it is necessary to transform conditional remarks into clear, direct statements. To respond, "I *might* say . . ." or "I *might* do . . ." tends to only cloud the issue and reinforce conditional tactics. What one might or could do always remains conjectural and frequently is at odds with actual behavior. In order that the therapy progress satisfactorily, obscure and conditional messages must be made explicit and nonconditional.

Two techniques used to force the client's strategy into the open are *direct confrontation* and *dare ploys*. *Direct confrontation* involves taking whatever the client communicates conditionally and transforming it into a declarative comment about the relationship. Thus when the client says:

"I wonder what you'd think *if* I ever started crying in here?"

the therapist replies:

"I think you feel like crying in here."

This simple example of the immediacy rule can be applied to a variety of contents, e.g., I wonder what you'd think if I _____ yelled? . . . cursed? . . . got up and left?, etc.

Dare ploys are similarly designed to transform the client's conditional remarks into direct interpersonal statements. Reflected in "Put your money where your mouth is" types of challenges, they tend to be most useful when the client's conditional comments appear on the verge of being expressed. Thus, when the client remarks:

"I wonder what you'd think if I got angry with you?"

the therapist might respond:

"Why don't you try?"

or

"There's only one way to really find out."

Both responses represent a goad to action designed to transform the client's conditional musings into action or at least into some form of active declaration.

In sum, the goal in Stage Two is to transform vague and conditional versions of the dependency, sexuality, and martyr strategies into unambiguous declarations so that the therapist can deal with them directly. To better appreciate how this occurs, we will consider each of these three strategies separately.

Dependency

The *dependency strategy,* described in Chapter 2, subsumes a
series of communicative maneuvers designed to solicit unending guidance and support. In the second stage of therapy, these strategies are
expressed via a continual stream of requests for help in making
decisions and resolving minor predicaments. Unlike the client's requests for advice and direction in Stage One, his attempts to solicit
support in Stage Two represent a massive effort to place the therapist
in the role of personal caretaker.

The use of dependency strategies often begins with "tidbit telling"—detailed reconstructions of the client's existence meant to involve the therapist in the farthest reaches of the client's life. In the
course of this development, the therapist finds that he is increasingly
asked to solve innumerable minor problems that crop up in the
client's everyday affairs. The greater proportion of these, however,
has little to do with whatever is going on in the treatment.

A clue to the irrelevant character of the client's story telling is
reflected in the trivial nature of the material that is brought up:

> One of the things Beth began doing after she concluded that
> psychotherapy had "changed her life" was to provide me with a
> picture of what it was like to be a buyer for a large department
> store. In one session after another, she recounted the details of
> her interactions with others in the organization, following this up
> with questions such as, "Do you think I should be nicer to
> _____ ?" and "What do you think about my future at
> _____ ?" "Do you think I said the right thing when [her
> immediate supervisor] said . . . ?"
>
> As the sessions progressed, it became increasingly obvious that
> Beth was interested more in placing me in the role of comforter
> and problem-solver than in self-exploration. A close examination
> of her questions and the situations over which they ranged sug-
> gested that she was not simply looking for temporary assistance
> in solving problems. She was looking for someone to lead her life
> for her!

As Stage Two progresses and the client monotonously recapitulates
life's minor trials and tribulations, the therapist often starts feeling
pestered, put upon, and annoyed. This is not unusual, since it is the
natural response for one who is on the receiving end of a dependency

strategy. Reactions such as these during the course of therapy simply attest to the fact that the strategy is operative and that the therapist has been selected as its target.

A common phenomenon in psychotherapies involving dependency strategies is the "extracurricular crisis." Phone calls in the middle of the night, requests for emergency appointments, and other requests of this sort become common and function to monopolize the therapist's time. An interesting feature of these "crises" is that they often do not involve anything approaching crisis proportions.

> Beth once telephoned in the midst of a session with another client to inform me about "something very important that had come up." The "crisis" turned out to be a letter from her younger sister who was having difficulties at home and asked to come live with Beth. Beth wasn't sure how to reply and felt an urgent need to consult with me. I assured her that the matter could wait until our next session, at which time we could discuss it in more detail. The subject of her younger sister, however, turned out not to be as urgent as the phone call had indicated. Beth failed to bring up the matter at all during the next session and when I questioned her about it, she casually remarked that she decided that she didn't want her kid sister living with her. She had in the interim written her sister a letter to this effect.

Implicit in such maneuvers, of course, is the client's communication that he needs constant emotional and intellectual support, support which only the therapist can provide. The goal of Stage Two is to force this message into the open and make it explicit.

Because of the dangers involved, the dependent client does not stand by passively and let this happen. He typically tries to orient the session to the past, starts talking of outside relationships, and retreats to relating tidbits or soliciting trivial advice. When this occurs, he should be forced via confrontation techniques or dare ploys to commit himself. Thus when the client says:

"What would you do *if* I asked you to help me with _____?"

the therapist must respond with:

"You'll have to ask to find out."

When the client says:

"I can't seem to make decisions without the help of (wife, husband, relative, friend, etc.),"

the therapist must respond:

"You seem to be asking *me* to _____ ."

If a dependency strategy is properly handled, Stage Two ends with a confession of helplessness on the client's part and the implicit or explicit demand for perpetual assistance. Often the client makes a remark in the nature of:

"The more I come here the more problems seem to crop up."

or

"I don't think I'll ever be able to make it on my own."

Through such comments, the client communicates to the therapist that he desperately needs him in order to get along. The more explicit this message becomes, the more readily the therapist can acknowledge the stage's completion.

Sexuality

Reliance on *sexual strategies* by individuals to structure their relationships is based on the assumption that erotic involvement alone holds the key to extended interpersonal commitment. Within psychotherapy, such strategies are depicted in the client's attempt to establish a relationship with the therapist solely through sexual means. The impetus for the client's behavior flows from his habitual use of sexual strategies outside therapy as well as from his experience in Stage One.

Sexual strategies are employed by both sexes, although they seem to enjoy more widespread use among women. When males employ sex in a strategic fashion, they do so primarily in verbal ways, such as through reports of sexual prowess. Females, in contrast, tend to rely more upon their bodies, although they too are quite adept at verbal eroticism. The presence of a sexual strategy in therapy usually is indexed by some combination of the following behaviors.

Detailed descriptions of promiscuous behavior
Hiking skirt or dress well up on thighs
Wearing suggestive clothing (low-cut or tight-fitting garments)*
Unsolicited descriptions of deep versus clitoral orgasm
Repeated references to restrictive sexual mores, etc.

There are, of course, many other ways in which a sexual strategy can make itself known. Perhaps the best subjective indication of its presence in the therapy is sexual arousal—on the part of the therapist. Explanations regarding transference and countertransference notwithstanding, most sexual strategists will have little difficulty arousing even the most "adjusted" therapist. Sex, after all, is the sexual strategist's stock in trade.

In the beginning portion of Stage Two, sexual strategies typically appear in the guise of double entendres, veiled insinuations, and ambiguous body movements. As the stage progresses, the seductive flavor of the interaction becomes more apparent. Somewhere along the way, many clients, for example, begin to show a "casual" interest in the therapist's marital relationships if he is married, or in the nature of his more general interchanges with members of the opposite sex. A common question asked by female clients in this stage is:

"I wonder how your wife feels about your talking to other women about intimate matters?"

If the client is not this bold as yet, she may phrase the same question by asking:

"I wonder how the wives of therapists feel about their talking to other women about intimate matters."

The reference to "other wives" and "other therapists" is, of course, an example of indirect and distanced dyadic communication and can be corrected through application of the "immediacy" rule.

As the stage continues and the client is brought more and more "into the room," conditional statements begin to appear. In discussing their past interactions, particularly those involving sexual escapades, many clients project the therapist into their stories by means of

---

* One of the author's clients who worked as an assembler in a toy factory came to the first few sessions of therapy in her work clothing—a bandana and dungaree "Rosie the Riveter" outfit. Later in the therapy, she did a dramatic turnabout and began attending sessions in a black, low-cut cocktail dress.

conditional communications. One client, telling of the difficulties she encountered because of her habit of rushing men into bed, interrupted her narrative with:

"I wonder how you'd react if I asked you up to my apartment?"

Comments such as this can be handled with some variant of a forcing technique in much the same way as the derivatives of other maladaptive strategies are. Direct confrontation, for instance, might result in something like:

"I think you're saying you'd like to ask me up to your apartment."

If the dare ploy is used, the therapist might respond:

"Are you sure you're just wondering?"

Both represent application of a Stage Two forcing technique to make explicit what is actually happening but is being merely alluded to.

Forcing a sexuality strategy into the open is obviously a risky operation, for both male and female therapists. It would be less than honest to deny that clients occasionally respond to direct confrontations with:

"I was only kidding; you really didn't take me seriously, did you?"

or

"What makes you think I'm interested in *you*?"

Direct confrontation, consequently, entails risking exposure of the sexual portion of one's ego, an ordeal that most persons, therapists notwithstanding, are not particularly eager to undergo. Beginning therapists can chart a safer course if they wish by initially sticking to dare ploys. This places the reponsibility for action in the client, and reduces the risk associated with the intervention. Whatever the case, the strategy must eventually be forced into the open if the therapy is to succeed.

Assuming that the client responds as expected and comes up with a declarative statement epitomizing what he or she has in mind, the end of Stage Two will be marked by a seduction overture. This is often spelled out in explicit fashion with the client actually proposing an after-hours rendezvous with the therapist. In some instances, however, it may be expressed less directly. A colleague related an episode in which a client asked him to drive her home after a particularly difficult session. She always took a taxi to and from therapy but this time claimed that she was "too bushed" to hunt for a cab. Earlier in the session, however, she had "accidentally" let it drop that her husband was away on a business trip.

The explicitness with which a sexual strategy, or any strategy for that matter, is spelled out largely depends upon what the therapist is comfortable with. As a general rule, though, the more explicit the better. A strategic maneuver that is open and direct is a maneuver that cannot be readily sidestepped, retracted or denied. This, as we will see in Stage Three, has important implications for how the strategy is dealt with.

Martyr

The final maladaptive strategy to be described is the *martyr strategy.* The use of this strategy is seen in the case of the housewife who "works her fingers to the bone" and the husband who "slaves all week at the office." As in the case of most martyr strategies, such communications contain the latent and desperate message: "Appreciate me!"

The presence of a martyr strategy in psychotherapy is revealed in the client's attempt to convince the therapist that he is an indispensable figure in the therapist's work. This often begins with the client complaining that no one understands him and that he is beginning to feel worse. Comments such as:

"I'm suffering more than ever."

"If someone only knew what I'm going through."

"I went through hell last week."

are common in this phase of treatment.

Expressions of this sort almost invariably leave the therapist feeling guilty about what he is putting the client through. Feelings of guilt, however, only validate the fact that the therapist has been targeted. Just as feelings of annoyance and sexual arousal, respectively, function as subjective indications of targeting in the dependency and sexuality strategies, so guilt feelings fulfill this role in the martyr strategy.*

The therapist once again deals with such statements by bringing them into the here and now:

"*I'm* making you suffer."

or

"You're saying that *I'm* making you miserable."

As the sessions progress, we hear the client remark that he could get better, he could do what the therapist wants him to do, if only the therapist would tell him what is supposed to happen. Although this sometimes is expressed in the client's feeble efforts to discuss the therapy process ("I've read Freud," "Will it help to analyze my dreams?", etc.), it passes quickly into a phase where the client indirectly offers to help the therapist become a better therapist. In an act of public-spirited devotion, the client relinquishes his claim to self-improvement in order that other patients may benefit from his experience. By offering himself up as a guinea pig, he symbolically declares that his only wish is to advance the therapist's career.

Some specific instances of the guinea pig ploy are represented in the following remarks by clients:

"Are you trying a technique? It's O.K. with me."

"How can I be more helpful?"

"I bet most of your patients wouldn't put up with this."

"I'm willing to try new things."

By declaring that he is willing to do anything in his power to help the therapist become more proficient, the client, in a subtle turnabout, reverses the helper-helpee roles. The client now is helping the therapist!

What does the client want in return? What does he seek in

---

* Sometimes guilt feelings also accompany dependency maneuvers. Nevertheless, dependency and martyr strategies are easy to differentiate, since the former involves requests for specific sorts of assistance while the latter involves a desire for appreciation.

payment for his "self-sacrifice?" "Only" appreciation—only some acknowledgment from the therapist that he is receiving greater professional fulfillment from his work with the client than he is from any other client. It is this demand that characterizes martyr strategies and highlights their presence in the therapy.

Toward the end of Stage Two, martyr strategies culminate in fairly explicit demands for appreciation. The client doggedly seeks to gain an admission from the therapist that it is he, the therapist, who has extracted major benefit from their collaboration. Often this is preceded by the client's testimony to the effect that he is greatly improved. He follows this up with:

"Admit you couldn't have gotten this far without my help."

"You really learned a lot, didn't you?"

"Did you ever get this far with other patients?"

"I bet you've worked with some real uncooperative patients in your time."

Unlike the previous two strategies discussed, martyr strategies tend to be expressed fairly directly and therefore require little forcing. If forcing is needed, it can be accomplished with very little difficulty. The completion of Stage Two, in any case, is indexed by an explicit expression of what the client wants from the therapist—in the case of the martyr, appreciation.

Stage Two, as we have seen, is the stage in which the client's dominant strategy first appears in full force. The rules of this stage are designed to highlight the operation of the various strategies and to bring them out into the open. The rationale for this will soon become apparent. For the moment, though, some general comments about Stage Two operations seem in order. For one, the therapist in Stage Two must be careful not to deny or refute whatever the client is doing. He must not, in other words, engage in interpretation. To tell the client that he is manipulating others only slows down the therapeutic process and prevents the strategy from reaching its ultimate expression.

Second, the rules of this stage should be employed only if necessary. A strategy, as indicated earlier, develops in a somewhat autonomous fashion and will in many cases eventually make itself explicit without prompting. The therapist can strike a relatively passive pose, resorting to direct confrontation and dare ploys only when there seems to be a lag or block in the progression we described.

Finally, the therapist must be careful not to fall into the trap of gratifying the client's strategic demands. Ethical matters aside, responding to the client's seductive overtures, for example, only functions to reinforce the strategy. This is seen in the account of a female patient who tells of her sexual involvement with her therapist, Bill:

> I feel that my therapeutic relationship with Bill would have been a hell of a lot more profitable for me if he would've tuned into what I was doing. I was seducing him. Which was being cute, which was being all these things to get him to like me. So I couldn't be honest with him. Just as I couldn't be when I was fucking with him, I couldn't be in the relationship with him because I was trying to gain. It's the same thing. I don't know why he didn't notice it, but we didn't deal with it at all. So I was accomplishing my neurotic goal when my problem was having an honest relationship with a man. Even in a therapeutic relationship I wasn't able to be honest. (Shepard, 1971, p. 75)

As the excerpt demonstrates, "success" of a strategy does not bode well for the success of the psychotherapy.

Similar examples could be found to demonstrate the negative effects of complying with the demands implicit in other maladaptive strategies. Submitting to the dependent strategist's demand for nurturance, for example, places the therapist continually "on call," something that is tremendously time-consuming. And feeding into the demands of the martyr is tantamount to an admission that the therapist is incapable of helping patients who are unwilling to cooperate— a rather devastating admission for the therapist who wishes to work with highly resistant patients such as schizophrenics or sociopaths. Capitulating to the demands implicit in any of the maladaptive strategies usually signals the strategy's success and the therapy's failure.

In Stage Two, in sum, the client asks for a commitment that goes beyond that of the original therapy contract. Because of the interpersonal risk associated with such a request, the client's strategic communications are initially phrased in vague and cryptic ways. It is the therapist's task in Stage Two to transform the client's vague communicative gestures into clear, unambiguous statements. The explicit version of each strategy, whether a seductive overture, declaration of helplessness, or demand for appreciation, constitutes the behavioral shift of the stage and the beginning of Stage Three.

STAGE THREE: STRIPPING

Stage Three represents a pivotal stage in the psychotherapy, since it is the phase of the process in which the client's strategy is confronted and ultimately rendered useless. Although this represents a difficult procedure for therapist and client alike, it is a part of the process which cannot be avoided or mitigated. Before the client can learn to relate in adaptive ways, his strategy must be stripped of its functional utility.

In Stage Two the therapist allowed himself to be targeted so as to foster the development of the client's strategy. In Stage Three the therapist relinquishes this stance and directly challenges the client's use of maladaptive maneuvers. The result is a complex series of interchanges whose characteristics are dictated by a rule called *refutation-affirmation*.

Refutation-Affirmation

The rule that governs the therapist's behavior in Stage Three subsumes a series of techniques aimed at actively undermining strategic ploys. Labeled *refutation-affirmation,* it signifies the therapist's refusal to relate to the client on the client's terms while at the same time affirming his continued interest in the client's well-being. He initiates this sequence by abandoning the role of target and attacking the client's strategies through silences, sarcasm, and other techniques designed to directly deny the client's exploitive demands.

The client, as might be suspected, does not take all this lightly. Faced with the potential loss of his major means of dealing with people, he musters all the resources at his disposal to prevent the therapist from accomplishing his task. Instead of abandoning his strategic efforts, he intensifies them: the dependent strategist signals increased helplessness, the sexual strategist becomes more seductive, and the martyr concludes that perhaps he is not doing enough.

The therapist must take care not to capitulate, either by offering the client support or by engaging in interpretation. There is unfortunately no salient substitute for stripping and no way to avoid doing what has to be done. The only proper response to intensified strategic demands is to continue to refute, to continue to chip away at the client's maladaptive method of structuring the relationship.

An example of refutation is provided by the case of a client whose exploitive demands occurred in the context of a dependency strategy. The case involved a female graduate student who had sought treatment after a series of broken engagements. A young woman in her early twenties, she had quietly confessed to the therapist at the end of Stage Two that she could not go on without his help. In Stage Three, her behavior was characterized by a stream of requests for direction and support. We join her in one of the later sessions in the stage:

> *Cl:* You won't believe some of the silly things that bug me. Chuck insists on flats and I don't give in. (Chuck is an old family friend whom the client occasionally dates.)
>
> *Th:* What?
>
> *Cl:* Chuck keeps asking me not to wear heels on dates. I guess it's because he's kind of short and ... anyway it annoys him. It's not unreasonable but I just don't like flats. What do you think I should do?
>
> *Th:* You want me to decide whether you should wear flats or heels?
>
> *Cl:* Sort of ... I guess so.
>
> *Th:* Doesn't it strike you as kind of silly, our spending time discussing what kind of shoes you should wear?

The client responded to this with a coquettish giggle and a sheepish grin. Undaunted, she continued:

> *Cl:* My mother always told me what to wear; I always thought that when I was on my own, I'd be happy to choose for myself. *(Pause)* Anyway, that's not important. She called last week ... asked me to come home for the Thanksgiving holidays. I've been thinking about it all week. I've been meaning to ask you what you think of the idea.
>
> *Th:* I have the feeling that you'd make up some problem for me if one didn't actually exist.

It is clear that the client could have been offered help in solving her predicament. The therapist could have explored the implications of the client's going home or focused perhaps on the nature of her dependent relationship with her mother. Given the goals of this stage, however, this would not have been particularly productive. Interpretation, since it is a form of help-giving, would at this point have functioned only to reinforce the client's dependent maneuvers.

Another example of refutation is seen in the context of a sexuality strategy. The passage below followed an exchange in which a client asked the author to have dinner with her so that "you could get to know me better." This was followed by a long silence broken by the client.

Cl: Well?
Th: I'm flattered by the invitation, but I don't think much good would come of it.
Cl: *(after a brief pause)* How do you know?
Th: I want to know you. ... I think there's more to you than just getting in your pants.
Cl: Who said that . . .?
Th: *(interrupting the client)* Let's not play games.
Cl: *(after a lengthy pause)* Where do we go from here?

The matter did not end there. The client tried on subsequent occasions to arrange "extracurricular" meetings, using as her rationale the idea that it would further the therapy. Throughout all these episodes, it was necessary to decline with a firm "Thanks, but no thanks," in the face of vehement contentions that I was aloof and uncaring.

Continued refutation often leads to violent personal attacks marked by sobbing, shouting, and sometimes even depression. Along the way, the therapist is subjected to accusations that take the form of:

Cl: You treat me like an object!

Cl: Who told you you could help anyone!

Cl: You've only made things worse.

Cl: You sadistic S.O.B.

and so on. Feeling rejected, helpless, and inept, the client directs his wrath at the person who obviously is responsible for making him feel this way, for divesting him of his strategy.

At this point in the process, an interesting development called *pseudotermination* often occurs. Many clients, assuming that therapy has come to an end, either make some comment to this effect or simply notify the therapist that they will not be coming any more. In their hurt and confusion, they mistake the annihilation of their strategy for the annihilation of the relationship.

When this happens, it is necessary to affirm the relationship. The therapist does this by emphasizing his commitment to the client and the treatment process. This involves telling the client that the psychotherapy is not over, that he is expected to remain in treatment, and that the therapist will stick by him during this difficult period.

Nevertheless, many clients conclude that the therapist is only trying to placate them. Convinced that the therapy is, in fact, over, they believe that the therapist is simply biding his time until an advantageous moment arrives to terminate the relationship. In such instances, the relationship can be affirmed by indicating that the therapy hour will continue to be held open for the client in the future as it always has in the past. Statements such as:

Th: I'll be here for our appointment next week.

or

Th: I'm keeping this hour open for you.

usually suffice, since it is the therapist's time rather than his promises for cure or improvement that behaviorally validate his commitment to the client.

The therapist must take care not to mitigate the client's difficulty (or his own) by making statements such as, "Why don't you try coming for just a few more weeks?" or "Things will get better." The client's decision to remain in therapy at this point requires him to take a substantial risk for perhaps the first time in his life. He finally is faced with investing himself in a relationship where he is highly vulnerable without the benefit of his customary strategic maneuvers. This is a harrowing experience, one which cannot be tempered by verbal palliatives.

As indicated earlier, this phase of therapy is also difficult for the therapist. Faced with a chagrined, frustrated and frightened individual, the therapist does not know from moment to moment whether the client will stay in treatment. It is for this reason that the psychotherapy process was initiated with "hooking." The procedures in Stage One were designed to tip the scale in favor of the client's remaining in treatment through this difficult period, a precaution whose significance could not be appreciated until Stage Three of the therapy process was reached. If the first two stages have been successfully negotiated, the odds are that the client will decide to remain.

An example of a refutation-affirmation sequence is described by Frieda Fromm-Reichman in *Principles of Intensive Psychotherapy* (1950). Working with a schizophrenic patient, she describes his tremendous resistance to all attempts on her part to get close to him.* Through persistent efforts, though, she managed to make some inroads. The patient, however, was extremely ambivalent about these developments and in a massive gesture of fright and denial he smeared feces on her. Refusing to respond to the patient's attempt to sever the relationship, Fromm-Reichman arrived the next day in a laboratory coat which could be easily laundered! This classic example of refutation-affirmation vividly portrays the extremes to which some people will go to negate a relationship and the extremes to which others will go to affirm it. The end of Stage Three, while typically portrayed in less dramatic ways, nevertheless ends with a refutation-affirmation sequence structurally similar to the one just described.

Although stripping procedures culminate in a termination statement with most clients, with some it leads to new sorts of maladaptive behavior. Some clients maintain secondary as well as primary strategies, and when the more dominant one fails, the secondary strategy often takes its place. When this occurs, the therapist is faced with a whole new series of maladaptive maneuvers, presenting him with the *deja vu* sensation that he is back at the beginning of Stage Two.

The presence of dual strategies, while not common, is not rare. Their operation outside therapy can be observed, for example, in the behavior of the overprotective ("martyr") mother. Continually sacrificing herself for her children, she is the type of woman who runs into difficulty when her children mature and start to leave the home. Some mothers may try to forestall their loss by falling back on a dependency strategy. Unable to structure their relationship in martyric ways, they signal helplessness via "I'll die without you" types of communications.

The appearance of dual strategies in psychotherapy is often interpreted by the beginning therapist as a sure sign that he has

---

* The reader will recall that the schizophrenic's extreme distancing maneuvers represent *his* maladaptive strategy.

created "new pathology." This, however, is a mistaken impression, since the secondary strategy is not particularly new; it has always been present as a latent behavioral element in the client's repetoire, held in reserve precisely for situations such as this. The fact that it makes its presence known at this point bears testimony to the therapist's success in stripping the primary strategy.

The client's secondary strategy should be handled in much the same way as was his dominant strategy. Operationally, this means that some preceding stages in treatment must be repeated, an operation referred to earlier as *looping*. Looping involves returning to an earlier point in the treatment process and repeating what has already been done on different content. If, for example, a dependency strategy appears at the end of Stage Three after a dominant martyr strategy has been extinguished, the therapist must return to the beginning of Stage Two and repeat what has been done in Stage Two and Three—this time on dependency maneuvers.

Dealing with secondary strategies is, nevertheless, usually an easier task than dealing with primary strategies. First, the dyadic framework of the therapy has already been set. The need to devote a great deal of time and energy in establishing the "here and now" context is thus somewhat obviated. Second, the strength of the subsidiary strategy and the skill with which it is employed are not as great. Since the secondary strategy is much less established in the client's behavioral repetoire, it is consequently much less difficult to strip.

An example of dual strategies in therapy was observed in the case of Beth. Beth's dependency strategy, first hinted at in the mother-daughter relationship with the older lesbian and later in her behavior vis à vis the therapist, constituted her primary means of dealing with people. Her secondary strategy, sexuality, occurred only when the primary one faltered.

The following sequence revolved about a refutation episode in Stage Three in which Beth's dependency maneuvers were clearly in focus. The sequence occurred after her help-seeking was responded to negatively for two successive weeks. This particular episode developed out of an interchange which began with Beth's relating a number of trivial incidents.

> *Th:* It's as if you come to each session with a little shopping bag full of troubles and pick them out for me one at a time.

> Beth: Isn't that what I'm supposed to do? I thought that's what you were interested in.
> Th: I'm interested in *you*.
> Beth: *(begins softly sobbing)*
> Th: *(offers a tissue which the client takes)*
> Beth: *(still sobbing)* I need your help so much and you don't seem to want to give it.
> Th: *(sarcastically)* You poor, poor thing.
> Beth: *(now crying violently and shouting)* You're killing me, you bastard . . . you're destroying me . . .

This sequence was followed by about ten more minutes of crying, after which the client dried her tears and composed herself.

> Beth: *(softly)* Does it pay for me to keep coming?
> Th: I'll be here next week . . . same time, same place.
> Beth: I'm not sure I'll be coming.
> Th: You decide what's best. Just remember, this time is yours; I'll be here no matter what you decide.
> Beth: *(walking out the door)* Don't expect me.

Beth returned for her next scheduled appointment acting as if nothing unusual had happened in the last session. At the very end of therapy, she reminisced about this portion of the treatment and confessed that she has spent "a hellish week" prior to her return. At first she convinced herself that I had given up on her and had given her appointment time to another client. She nevertheless decided to just "drop by," and felt tremendously relieved to find me waiting for her.

In subsequent sessions, the content of our interchanges shifted as Beth began describing a series of past and present sexual escapades in minute detail. It was obvious from her careful descriptions that they were meant not to provide information so much as to titillate. During one of these sessions, Beth described a date which culminated in heavy petting with a young male undergraduate. In the course of her narration, she provided a detailed description of a clitoral masturbation sequence. After she finished her account, I challenged her with:

> Th: Why all the details? Were they all really necessary?
> Beth: You never seemed bothered by details before.
> Th: But you could have just told me you petted with the guy and left it at that.
> Beth: *(emphatically)* I just thought that you should know.

> Th: (after more questioning of this sort) I think you were just trying to get me hot.
> Beth: (in a half-suprised, half-joking tone) You dirty old lecher.
> Th: They're *your* stories.
> Beth: (now getting very serious) You're crazy!
> Th: They're your stories and they're very sexy.
> Beth: (angrily) Let's change the subject; I don't want to talk about it any more.

Since the session was almost over, the matter was not pursued. In the next session, the client said that she had been thinking about what had happened and thought maybe I wasn't so crazy. She continued by asking whether I would meet her for a drink afterwards in order that I might get a "better picture" of her:

> Th: Where?
> Beth: How about _____ ? (the name of a local gay bar)
> Th: And we could talk privately there?
> Beth: We could have a drink or two and then go somewhere else.
> Th: For instance?
> Beth: (after a moderate pause) My place is quiet.
> Th: Listen to me carefully, Beth. I'm not going to sleep with you.
> Beth: (in a muffled, depressed tone) Why do you keep seeing me?
> Th: That's what you're going to have to find out. Why do I keep seeing you if I don't want to screw you.

It is instructive to note that Beth did not become extremely upset during this refutation episode. Since the second refutation occurs on the heels of an earlier affirmation experience, it tends to be less traumatic. As in the case of most clients who employ dual strategies, Beth was less disturbed about strategic rejection this time than she was when it occurred the first time.

Whether Stage Three ends with a single refutation-affirmation sequence or in looping, the effect is the same. The client, anxious and often depressed, concludes that the psychotherapy is coming to an end and that the therapist wants nothing more to do with him. He nonetheless must deal with residual PnP motivation developed in Stage One and the therapist's declaration of continued commitment.

The client's resolution of this dilemma marks an important milestone in the treatment process and forms the basis for the type of learning that is to take place in stage four.

STAGE FOUR:
ADAPTIVE STRATEGIES

The interpersonal acceptance that accompanies stripping constitutes the most salient learning experience in the entire psychotherapy process. The client has been psychologically exposed in a close relationship and has found, to his amazement, that the relationship has survived. If the relationship is to continue, however, new ground rules must be set. And it is largely the client's task to discover what these are.

In Stage Four, the client must figure out how to maintain a profitable relationship without the benefit of his trustworthy interpersonal maneuvers. It is in this stage that the client first learns to relate in a manner other than that dictated by his maladaptive strategy. This does not mean, however, that he suddenly starts to behave in adaptive ways. Adaptive strategies, like maladaptive ones, evolve over a long period of time and develop through a series of extended relationships. Stage Four merely lays the foundation for the future development of such strategies; their full development occurs largely after the therapy is concluded.

The transactions that constitute Stage Four are designed to help the client recognize patterns in his current behavior which ultimately lead to social debacles. For perhaps the first time in his life, he is afforded the opportunity to see how his behavior affects others and prevents him from maintaining meaningful relationships. It is the client's recognition of his own social stimulus value, beginning with an analysis of his impact on the therapist, that constitutes one of the major yields of the psychotherapy.

Stage Four begins with the client's "return" to therapy and his fledgling attempts to maintain the relationship on some basis other than that dictated by his maladaptive strategy. Some clients, unable to believe that what is happening is on the level, frequently begin the stage by challenging the therapist's motives. They may, for example, insist that the therapist persists in seeing them only because it is his job or because he needs the money. It is easy to dispose of such

arguments simply by telling the patient that other clients also have
money or, if one is working in a hospital or clinic, that other patients
are available to fill the client's time slot. Whatever arguments the
client presents, the fact that the therapist continues to see him week
after week is by itself de facto evidence of the therapist's dyadic
investment.

In the course of ensuing sessions, the client searches for ways to
structure the relationship; he may ask the therapist for suggestions or
he may search for things that seem profitable to discuss, but the end
result is the same: the client comes up with little more than "small
talk." After a session or two of this, the client finally begins to give of
himself by divulging very personal information, information so personal that it never has turned up before in the therapy; the client
begins to engage in *risky revealing*.

Some examples of the kinds of things clients reveal in this stage
are as follows:

A phobic client tells of fear of progressive and irreversible mental illness—fears which began much before the onset of the
phobia.

A frigid woman tells how she conned her husband into marriage
and of her intense fear of getting close to him, due to her concern
that such a move might lead to rejection.

A young college student confides his deep concern that he is a
latent homosexual.

A multiple divorcée reveals her thoughts that *she* is responsible
for the breakups and that no one would want to stay married to
her.

A woman with a disturbed daughter and a deteriorating marriage reveals her conviction that something in her hereditary or
psychological makeup "caused" her daughter's disturbance.

Added to these are secret murderous or incestuous impulses which
the client has never before told anyone, not even his closest confidant.

The things that people tell their therapist in this phase of treatment are far-ranging. The character of these revelations, however,
differ from the types of admissions clients make in the initial stages of

treatment. In this stage, disclosures have more to do with profound fears and deep feelings of worthlessness than with specific behavioral deficiencies. Jourard (1964), in his preface to *The Transparent Self,* writes:

> I became fascinated with the phenomenon of self-disclosure after puzzling about the fact that patients who consulted me for therapy told me more about themselves than they had ever told another living person. Many of them said, "You are the first person I have ever been completely honest with." (p. iv)

A similar sentiment is reflected in a letter received by the author from an ex-client. It read, "I don't know whether any other human being will ever know me as well as you."

Whatever the precise nature of the material revealed, risky revealing represents the client's unique attempt to extend himself in a relationship as he never has before. The client's "offering," so to speak, marks perhaps *the* first time that he has ever risked himself in a relationship. It is the risking rather than the content of the revelation, per se, that constitutes a significant development in the treatment process.

How can the therapist repay the client? By analyzing the basis for his concerns? By trying to convince him that his feelings of worthlessness are unwarranted? Neither of these solutions is particularly effective, since feelings of this sort are not easily dealt with through intellectual analysis. Perhaps counterrevelation is the key? Hardly. The introduction of counterrevelation implicitly presumes the promise of a long-term commitment, something for which the current relationship holds little potential. What, then, can the therapist do to reinforce the client's fledgling attempts at taking interpersonal risks? The answer lies in a form of interactional revealing that centers about the therapist's immediate experiential response to the client. Labeled "transactional feedback," it constitutes the psychotherapeutic rule of Stage Four.

Transactional Feedback

The type of response generated by the transactional feedback rule subsumes a series of direct, no-holds-barred reactions to the client as a human being. Since the physical and verbal idiosyncracies associated with the client's maladaptive strategy do not magically

disappear at the end of Stage Three, the therapist is given the opportunity in Stage Four to respond to the client in such a way as to make
him aware of what he does to undermine relationships. Transactional
feedback, in short, focuses on the specific behaviors that constitute
the client's strategic maneuvers.

This portion of treatment sees the therapist comment on the
ways in which the client habitually executes his strategy, with particular reference to the way it affects the therapist. Examples of the kinds
of things the therapist is likely to comment upon are:

    Belligerent mannerisms
    Seductive posturing
    Pained facial expressions
    Gabbiness
    Withdrawal maneuvers (excessive silences, eye wandering, etc.)
    Vocal quality (chip-on-the-shoulder tone, whineyness, etc.)

The reader can easily complement this list with examples from his
own work.

The specific way in which the therapist responds to all of this
obviously depends on his personal style. Some therapists couch their
feedback in phrases such as, "Do you know that you have a tendency
to _____?" Others tend to be more blunt and direct, in which case
comments such as "You really turn me off when you _____" are
more common. Whatever course is adopted, it should be noted that
the therapist's response—tactful or tactless, mild or harsh—probably
would have resulted in the client's alienation and possible termination
had it occurred early in the treatment process. In this stage, it is
accepted and assimilated.

Some examples of the types of interchanges generated by the
transactional feedback rule are given below. The first regards a dependent male client who experienced many difficulties in his initial
contacts with people:

    Th: You look like you're going to burst out crying.
    Cl: (surprised) What do you mean?
    Th: You're so tense and you've got such a sad look on your
          face. You look like you're going to either explode or start
          crying.
    Cl: I was just thinking of something.

> *Th:* But it makes me uncomfortable just sitting next to you when you look like that.

This next example involves a woman whose history also was characterized by dependency ploys:

> *Cl:* *(after talking nonstop for almost fifteen minutes)* And when I meet a new person I'm bubbly on the outside, but inside I know there's nothing. One time I almost came out with a horrible shriek ... but I knew they would take me away and that would be the end.
>
> *Th:* I have the feeling you honestly want me to listen to *what* you're saying.
>
> *Cl:* *(momentarily taken aback)* Of course I do; what kind of a remark is that?
>
> *Th:* It's hard for me to pay attention to what you're actually saying because your voice is so whiney.
>
> *Cl:* *(pause)* I guess it's gotten to be such a habit, I don't even notice it anymore.

As difficult as these interchanges are for the client, they provide him with important information about the way he affects people. The "only-your-best-friend-will-tell-you" aspect of the interaction, moreover, tends to reinforce the risky revealing which preceded it.

In the case of Beth, transactional feedback was used first in a session immediately following one in which she disclosed lifelong feelings of difference and worthlessness. In this and subsequent sessions, the discussion focused upon her dependent and sexual behavior.

> Beth's use of dependency tactics was depicted most saliently in her presentation of herself as a pathetic, downtrodden figure. In response to this, I repeatedly pointed out how her demeanor, that of a weak, helpless person, led to feelings of pity on my part and how such feelings could hardly be expected to form the basis for mutually profitable relationships. In the process I noted such things as her tendency to lower her voice when speaking of personal accomplishments, her habit of looking down when talking about her past, and other mannerisms which set a tone of infirmity and helplessness with others.

Feedback regarding Beth's sexual patterns took many forms, one example of which is depicted in the following exchange:

> Beth: *(dejectedly)* I used to date guys fairly often but none ever stayed interested in me for very long.
>
> Th: You know, I have the feeling that I wouldn't ask you out more than a couple of times if I started dating you.
>
> Beth: *(nodding head as if this didn't surprise her)* Why?
>
> Th: For one, you come on too fast, you'd probably scare me. And the other thing is I'd have to figure out what to do with you when we weren't screwing.
>
> Beth: *(indignantly)* But I'm interested in other things ... in having a home and family like everyone else.
>
> Th: Did you ever tell this to anyone?
>
> Beth: *(eyes downcast, she shakes her head)* No.

Through such exchanges, Beth was exposed to a type of information that heretofore had been unavailable to her. Although such feedback was often painful, it provided her with an opportunity to see how she was viewed through the eyes of another human being.

The initial response to transactional feedback, usually one of astonishment, is typically followed by attempts to tie what is happening in therapy to interactions outside of it. Feedback transactions now function as the bridge that carried the client to his relationships outside of treatment:

> Toward the end of Stage Four, Beth was beginning to relate the feedback she received to various incidents outside of therapy. She told, for example, how on first dates she would unabashedly reveal intimate details about herself, her relationship with her parents, and her painful experiences in boarding school—all to men whom she knew only superficially. She also told of how she used sex on numerous occasions to salvage relationships presumed to be faltering. Operating on the assumption that early self-disclosure and/or promiscuity held the key to greater involvement, she had no inkling of the fact that her own actions invariably led to the demise of potentially promising relationships.

The end of Stage Four, consequently, is marked by a tendency on the client's part to relate the feedback he or she receives to past interpersonal fiascos with particular reference to intimate relationships.

Although the tendency of the client to discuss extratherapy occurrences at this point is significant, it tends to overshadow what is, in effect, the major behavioral change of this stage. The client, by engaging in risky revealing *and* by using the therapist for feedback purposes, has begun to adopt some of the maneuvers that comprise adaptive strategies. It is this, rather than understanding or "insight," that constitutes the primary shift in Stage Four. Nevertheless, the "turning outward" of the therapy constitutes a concrete indication that Stage Four has come to a close.

STAGE FIVE:
UNHOOKING (TERMINATION)

The fifth and final stage of interactional psychotherapy sees the dissolution of the client-therapist relationship. The reader will recall that the procedures of Stage One (hooking) were designed to imbue the therapist with a utility he did not initially possess, a utility born of the need to fulfill PnP. This formed the foundation for the transactions that took place in the middle stages of treatment, in which the client was exposed to a series of potent learning experiences. In the final stage, the client's investment in the therapist must be withdrawn. The client must be extricated from the relationship, unhooked so to speak, so that he is able to form productive relationships outside of therapy.

Unhooking in interactional psychotherapy is not a particularly difficult procedure. This cannot be said for all therapies. There are many psychotherapies that drone on monotonously year after year simply because the therapist has become too much of a fixture in the client's life or because the therapist cannot let go. The likelihood of this occurring in interactional psychotherapy, however, is slim. First, risky revealing and transactional feedback tend to be self-limiting operations. Since one can only reveal so much about himself and because feedback is finite, the utility of the therapist decreases with each additional session after the completion of Stage Four. Second, the growth of selfish altruism as the client's means of dealing with people leads to attempts on his part to enhance the role-functioning of the therapist. In the context of psychotherapy, paradoxically, the only way he can do this is to terminate treatment! This is the only behavioral way the client can testify to the therapist's effectiveness.

Because the impetus for termination resides in the client rather than in the therapist, Stage Five contains no new therapist rule. Although the therapist may offer support, and even push the client a bit if he procrastinates, the ultimate responsibility for termination lies with the client.

The initial transactions of Stage Five are generally quite awkward, often characterized by long periods of silence, small talk, and dead-end discussions. Whereas earlier in treatment the client had no difficulty finding something to discuss, he now has to search about for a meaningful topic. The client's inability to engage the therapist, a sure sign of avoidance earlier in therapy, is now interpreted in an entirely different light. In Stage Five, this inability is construed as a legitimate response to the waning utility of the therapist.

The awkward period that initiates Stage Five usually does not last long. Eventually, the client begins making remarks concerning termination. He wonders whether he can "make it on his own," whether he "needs the therapist anymore," and so on. Remarks commonly overheard in this phase of treatment are:

> *Cl:* Can you give me an idea of how much longer I have to come?

and

> *Cl:* Do you think I have to come *every* week?

The implicit message contained in each, the wish to terminate, is a valid one and should not be interpreted as some sort of defense. If the patient desired to escape, he could have done so earlier when he had good reason to. In this stage of treatment, the desire to terminate is a healthy sign and should be supported.

But matters are not always this simple. Patients, being ignorant of theory, do not always conform to it. A number of patients find it difficult to sever their bond with the therapist and tend to put off termination. In such instances, it may be necessary to facilitate unhooking via remarks such as:

> *Th:* We used to have more to say to each other.

> *Th:* Your thoughts seem to be someplace else nowadays.

or, more directly, by comments such as:

Th: I have the feeling you've been thinking of stopping.

Th: *(in a friendly tone)* Don't you have anything better to do with this hour?

The last remark was directed at Beth. She responded by gleefully jumping from her chair and remarking:

"Yep, but I wanted to see how long it would take you to get to it."

She left after a few more minutes of conversation and did not return until six months later, when she dropped in for a brief social visit.

Regardless of the precise manner in which the issue of termination is broached, the therapy should be brought to completion as soon as possible after termination is considered. The therapist's continued attempts to insure generalization (making inside-to-outside connections) and conduct postmortems ("Let's review what happened") only serve to communicate to the client that the therapist may harbor lingering doubts about the client's readiness to strike out on his own.

The fact of the matter is that no one is really ever ready to strike out "on his own." This is why interactional therapy ends not in a reconstructed personality or in emotional insight as much as it does in "seeking." The client, having learned what it means to truly encounter and use another human being, leaves therapy with the intention of seeking out and building meaningful relationships with people who can gratify his needs.

The client's efforts to establish a gratifying relationship with some new person or to cultivate one with someone who already exists in his life-space constitutes the generalization mechanism of the interactional approach. A dyadic void has been created with the completion of the termination stage, and the client, still motivated by PnP, seeks to fill it. The difference is that now he is armed with a different set of interpersonal tools. These tools, developed in an atmosphere of intimacy and commitment, form the rudimentary beginnings of adaptive ways of relating. To the extent that one grows in the context of his ongoing relationships, the end of interactional therapy represents the beginning rather than the end of a significant interpersonal growth process.

SUMMARY AND CONCLUSIONS

Interactional psychotherapy comprises a five-stage behavioral change process based on a series of experiential exchanges between client and therapist. Focusing on the here-and-now character of the dyadic interaction, the process relies upon the therapist's use of himself as the medium of therapeutic change. The precise change sequence grows out of rules which guide the therapist's behavior, which in turn are largely responsible for the movement, or behavioral shifts, of the client.

Reviewing the five stages indicates that their constituent rules are essentially reactive in nature. Except for the hint of an interpretive rule in Stage Four (where "inside-outside" associations are made), interpretive rules are conspicuously absent in this particular therapy process. The fact that interactional therapy lacks such rules, however, should not be surprising. Any therapy that pins its hopes for change on action rather than insight, on experience rather than understanding, will be represented for the most part through reactive rules.

It should also be apparent that many of the operations described in this chapter are not unique to the interactional approach. Many systems include stages comparable to hooking and unhooking, and a great proportion employ confrontation techniques. This, perhaps, is simply another way of acknowledging that the critical dimension in most forms of psychotherapy is the client-therapist relationship. Thus, Edward Bordin, a prominent psychotherapy researcher, writes:

> The key to the influence of psychotherapy on the patient is in his relationship with the therapist. Wherever psychotherapy is accepted as a significant enterprise, this statement is so widely subscribed to as to become trite. Virtually all efforts to theorize about psychotherapy are intended to describe and explain what attributes of the interactions between the therapist and the patient will account for whatever behavior change results. (1959, pg. 235)

The stages outlined in this chapter represent one of these efforts.

Whether one wishes to follow the interactional approach as set down or to select only those stages which are most useful is, of course, an individual decision. Whichever path is chosen, the important thing to keep in mind is that a system's integrity is inextricably tied to the theory which spawns it and to the stages that comprise it.

Consequently, different stages and operations cannot be combined merely because they "fit well" or because they lead to occasional "cures." In order to accurately gauge what contributes to therapeutic success, it is necessary to specify as carefully as possible one's basic assumptions regarding therapeutic change. It is the presence of a guiding theoretical formulation, operationally expressed through a sequence of behavioral stages, that provides the consistency and continuity that form the basis for therapeutic growth.

Finally, the emphasis on stages and rules should not obviate the fact that psychotherapy is an altogether human enterprise. Sometimes the nature of the enterprise forces the therapist to do things he might not do in ordinary relationships, such as engage in extended confrontation. But the basic element, that of caring for another human being, underlies his every intervention. The fact that the therapist develops certain principles of therapeutic functioning does not necessarily mean that he embraces a mechanistic view of psychotherapy. Rather, it reflects his willingness to take a close, hard look at the ways in which he influences others. And this places him in a better position to maximize his encounter with the client by making his interventions more relevant and effective.

The reader who has some familiarity with groups will have realized that what has been described in this chapter is not unique to individual psychotherapy. Groups, whether they be family, sensitivity, or traditional psychotherapy groups, are highly interactional affairs. They invariably deal with failures to develop and maintain meaningful relationships. In the final chapter, we turn to a consideration of group approaches, using as an organizing principle the concept of strategic change.

5
Interactional Group Therapy

The use of groups for therapeutic purposes has grown at a phenomenal rate in the past few years. Although reports in the media suggest that group techniques, including encounter, sensitivity, marathon, and family groups, are recent developments, the use of groups is not particularly new. Pratt (1906) introduced group treatment at the turn of the century in trying to help tubercular patients deal with adjustment problems, while J. L. Moreno, coiner of the phrase "group psychotherapy," is said to have worked with groups in Vienna as early as 1910 (Ruitenbeek, 1970, p. 16). Even sensitivity groups were employed as far back as 1947. Nevertheless, until the 1950s, group psychotherapy remained an adjunct to individual therapy and was thought to be a secondary choice at best.

Current indications suggest that this is no longer the case. Groups are now considered by many to be the primary form of treatment and are being used more and more to treat not only symptoms but loneliness, alienation, and feelings of purposelessness. Apparently the group approach offers something that the individual approaches cannot. The purpose of this chapter is to explore what this something might be and to point out some of the major distinctions among the various types of groups in existence.

A survey of different group treatment procedures reveals almost as many different types of group therapy as individual therapies.

Thus, there is pschoanalytic group therapy (Foulkes and Anthony, 1957; Wolf and Schwartz, 1962), client-centered group therapy (Hobbs, 1951), transactional group therapy (Berne, 1963), a number of family approaches (Ackerman, 1966; Bell, 1961; Jackson, 1961; Satir, 1967), and a plethora of variations on the encounter-sensitivity theme (Bradford et al., 1964; Egan, 1970; Schutz, 1967).

As in the case of individual therapy, questions of procedure and technique also arise in groups. How often should a group meet? How active should the therapist be? Should the group therapist emphasize or de-emphasize his role as leader? In addition, questions regarding the combination or sequencing of individual and group treatment must also be answered. Should the client be "prepared" for group treatment by first going through individual therapy? Is it wise for the client to be in group therapy and individual therapy simultaneously?

The answers to such questions derive, in part, from the therapist's past or current experience with groups. Group treatment today is still largely an innovative enterprise; many of the things a group therapist does in his Thursday group are related more to what works in his Tuesday group than to hard-and-fast theoretical dictates. Nevertheless, there are certain superordinate principles which tend to regulate the transactions between the group therapist and the group members. These constitute the rules of group therapy.

It has been our contention that much of the concrete actions taken by psychotherapists derive from theoretical considerations codified in rules and expressed through the concept of a process. This holds for group treatment as well as for individual therapy. Just as the individual therapy process depends on one's basic view of individual functioning, so the group process is intimately tied to one's conception of a group.

In some group therapies, the group is viewed primarily as an agent of *personal* change. Problems are seen to lie within individual members, with the group merely functioning as the medium through which these problems are broached. Thus in psychoanalytic group therapy, as in classical psychoanalysis, repressed wishes remain "the problem" and the multiple transferences that arise in the group are used to bring these to the fore (Foulkes and Anthony, 1957). In the client-centered approach, unsymbolized experiences and the inability to actualize oneself constitute "the problem." Other individual-oriented groups operate on similar premises and, for want of a better phrase, are referred to collectively as "individual-in-the-group" approaches.

In other groups, the emphasis is on the group as an entity in its own right. Here, it is the overall *system,* abstractly portrayed as a series of nodal points and interconnecting linkages, that is the focus of change. Within this approach, changes in the nodal points (personality change in individual members) are subordinated to changes in the linkages (communication patterns, group bonds, forces of attraction, etc.). This is referred to as the "group dynamic" approach.

Interactional group therapy does not neatly conform to either of these patterns but falls somewhere in-between. To the extent that the interactional group tries to alter maladaptive strategies of specific individuals, it approximates an individual-in-the-group approach. At the same time, maladaptive strategies are dyadic events and can therefore be conceptualized as miniature systems. To the extent that one analyzes the bonds and communications comprising these systems, a group dynamics perspective is adopted. In the following pages an attempt is made to show how the two emphases complement each other in enacting strategic change.

THE INTERACTIONAL GROUP: ROLES AND SOCIAL BEHAVIOR

The basic characteristics of human beings do not change when the individuals become members of a group. Their behavior may become more complex and personal vulnerability may be heightened, but basic motives remain the same. Whether a person is in individual therapy or group therapy, he tends to be concerned with his impact on others and his ability to maintain profitable relationships.

The primary difference between dyadic and group functioning lies in the concept of a social role. A social role represents a behavioral automatism, a stereotyped way of behaving in situations where quick, appropriate responses are called for. Thus if a young child is struck by a peer, he is likely to immediately strike back, whereas he "instinctively" inhibits this response if struck by his father. The roles of "peer" and "son" obviously call for vastly different responses, even when precipitating conditions are identical.

Role behaviors, as the preceding example indicates, are not always congruent with personal feelings. The role behaviors that people enact are often at odds with their private, more personal responses. Such responses, if made public, could conceivably place a person in a precarious position, since they may reveal a side of him that he does not wish others to see. Role behaviors, at least in the presence of those with whom we are not very intimate, tend therefore to reflect only limited aspects of ourselves.

Optimal role functioning nevertheless requires the integration of public role responses with private, more intimate feelings. For example, men who adhere too rigidly to the strong, aggressive male role that tends to predominate in our culture often experience difficulty forming close, lasting relationships with women. The most effective husbands, teachers, lovers, and executives are people who are able to step outside their prescribed roles and share personal parts of themselves with those with whom they form extended relationships.

The concept of role gains increased importance in groups, since any single sequence of behavior on a member's part has multiple social implications. This is seen most clearly in family therapy. The way a family member behaves in one role always has implications as to how the remainder of the family perceives him in the other family roles he plays. Thus, a husband may shy away from open expression of tenderness and affection toward his wife for fear that this might undermine his role as father and family disciplinarian. Such persons may remain impassive throughout therapy in the face of moving emotional interchanges in order to maintain an "in charge" image. Similar examples could be offered in other groups where different types of intertwined role relationships exist.

Interactional group therapy, based on principles of interpersonal exchange, follows essentially the same path as its individual counterpart, with the added consideration that greater attention is devoted to the part that stereotyped role behaviors play. This necessitates the introduction of an extra stage in the process—a "role competency" stage—to deal with defensive roling. Generally speaking, the stages of the group process (and most of the operations within them) duplicate the individual therapy process. Specific changes have to do primarily with technical differences resulting from the fact that the therapist must deal simultaneously with more than one person.

In the following pages the interactional group process is outlined, with an emphasis on differences in working with groups and working with individuals. Since the group process is thought to be generic, examples from family therapy and sensitivity groups are used to supplement examples from traditional group therapy in describing certain stages. At the end of the chapter, special attention is devoted to the structural ways in which various groups differ. At that point we consider in detail how family and sensitivity groups are set apart from more traditional approaches.

THE INTERACTIONAL GROUP: BASIC PRINCIPLES

The group therapist, like any other professional who deals with more than one person at a time, adheres to certain principles of group functioning to help him achieve his goals. Of these principles, two stand out more than others. The first of these, labeled the *vesting principle,* requires the therapist to subordinate his relationship vis à vis the client to emerging client-client relationships. Yalom, in *The Theory and Practice of Group Psychotherapy* (1970), writes:

> The curative factors in group therapy are primarily mediated not by the therapist but by the other members, who provide the acceptance and support, the hope, the experience of universality, the opportunities for altruistic behavior, and the interpersonal feedback, testing and learning. (p. 83)

The rationale for this is based on the belief that a series of multiple client-client encounters—if properly programmed—yields greater gains than any single encounter the therapist can offer. The therapist's exchanges with specific members, accordingly, are reduced in frequency and intensity, and the client's interactions with his fellow members are relied upon as the medium of psychotherapeutic change.

What this essentially means is that the group members themselves function as surrogate therapists. In the course of treatment, it is they who are vested with the task of interpretation and confrontation. This does not mean, however, that the therapist is passive; rather, he guides the behavior of group members so that they do, in fact, act in therapeutic ways. By monitoring the various interchanges, the therapist functions as the orchestrator of the group process.

The other major principle of group functioning has to do with equalizing the movement of individual members. Referred to as the *pacing principle,* it derives its name from the therapist's efforts to insure that group members move at approximately the same rate.

Though certain individuals may move faster than others, the pacing principle stipulates that the group as a whole be on a roughly equal psychological footing at the completion of each stage.

The necessity of equalizing the movement of group members is unique to group treatment. It does not arise in individual therapy, where the therapist can regulate the time spent in any one stage to match the idiosyncracies of the client. When a therapist must deal simultaneously with six to ten different individuals, each of whom may progress at a different rate, it is important that individual movement be controlled. If it is not, rapid movement by some members may not be matched by others, and progression into subsequent stages will be experienced by the slower members as confusing and threatening. The pacing principle aims at minimizing this possibility by seeing that all members are roughly matched at the end of each stage before moving on to the next.

With the above considerations in mind, we turn to the specific stages that comprise group therapy. As indicated earlier, the stages of the group process generally replicate those of individual treatment, with the exception that an additional stage is included. Thus, the six stages of strategic therapy are:

Stage One: Hooking
Stage Two: De-roling
Stage Three: Maladaptive Strategies
Stage Four: Stripping
Stage Five: Adaptive Strategies
Stage Six: Unhooking (Termination)

Stage Two, de-roling, constitutes the extra stage in the process.

STAGE ONE: HOOKING

The first session of group psychotherapy is typically anxiety-provoking for most participants. Whether or not a prospective group member has been in treatment before, the idea of talking about one's problems in front of strangers is at best unsettling and at worst very frightening. Given the state of tense expectation that surrounds the first meeting, the therapist's immediate job is to allay anxiety, reduce uncertainty, and create a comfortable, accepting atmosphere.

There are several ways to accomplish this. One is to immediately

get everyone on a first-name basis. Another is to spend a large part of
the first meeting structuring ensuing sessions; some of the things that
might be discussed are clandestine meetings between group members,* physical aggression during the sessions, etc. Some group therapists "break the ice" by posing such questions as "Who was anxious
about coming today?" Whatever course is taken, the immediate goal
is to get the group to feel at ease and get them to feel they have
something to share with each other—even if that something is anxiety
over attendance.

Perhaps the one thing a therapist should avoid in the first session
is requiring group members to tell each other about their respective
"problems." Even when one or two members are disposed to "show
and tell," the therapist should deftly prevent them from going into
excruciating detail. If this precaution isn't observed, other members
may feel obligated to reciprocate in kind, only to find that they have
prematurely revealed much more than they intended to. The first
session, in short, should accentuate what is positive in the group
rather than what is pathological.

Once the group members feel moderately comfortable in each
other's company, they usually begin to spontaneously share biograph-
ical information with one another. More often than not, such exchanges begin with guarded and superficial remarks not unlike the
types of remarks people make to each other in passing encounters.
Thus, the members tell each other what they do for a living, where
they grew up, family circumstances, and so on. In the course of such
exchanges, personal problems and interpersonal difficulties—with
employers, parents, spouses, children, etc.—are increasingly alluded
to. This provides the therapist with the opportunity to utilize the
techniques associated with the hooking stage: advice-giving and emotional coupling.

The primary difference between the use of hooking techniques in
group treatment and in individual treatment lies in the vesting of such
techniques in the group instead of in the therapist. This is seen
perhaps most clearly in the way the therapist transfers the advising
function to the group in Stage One. Thus, if a member talks about his
difficulty in meeting girls, the therapist may ask the group to try
advising him on date-getting techniques; female members, in particu-

* Some group leaders prohibit these, while others merely request that they be
brought up in the group if they occur.

lar, might be called upon to volunteer suggestions. If a participant complains about his in-laws' interference with his marriage, the therapist may encourage other members to suggest ways in which they have successfully handled their in-laws. In one situation after another, the therapist deftly avoids giving advice himself so that the group members come to perceive the group itself as the primary advisory resource.

Specific advice need not have a direct relation to the precise problem that brings the client to therapy. Thus, a member who was in the midst of trying to negotiate a divorce but was confused about her legal rights was given the name of a divorce attorney by another member. A young mother troubled over unsuccessful attempts to treat her enuretic child was given the name of a behavior therapist by a person in the group whose child had been successfully treated by him for excessive thumb-sucking. Obviously, the group therapist himself could have offered such advice if he so wished. But since his goal is to imbue the group with rewarding properties, he distributes the advice-giving function among the various group members.

Emotional coupling is vested in the group in a similar manner. This is accomplished by encouraging members of the group to respond to the feeling tone of statements made by other members. It usually facilitates matters at first if the therapist models such behavior to set the tone for what he expects the group to do. Thus, whenever appropriate, he follows up the remarks of clients with comments similar to those used in individual therapy. Examples are:

It seems to me that you feel *sad* (or *happy,* or *upset*) when you talk about . . .

or

You get very *angry* whenever you mention . . .

After a few sessions the group usually begins to spontaneously incorporate this technique into its own functioning.

To insure that emotional coupling is experienced on an equitable basis, the therapist should make a special effort to direct coupling-type statements toward members who tend to shy away from involvement. Examples are:

Th: Do you *(directed at a reticent member)* know how Jack is feeling right now?

or

> *Th:*   What was the feeling you *(directed at a specific member)*
>   had when Sue was speaking about her mother?

By making sure that all the members are on an approximately equal
footing, i.e., by following the pacing principle, the therapist prevents
particular members from becoming isolated.

Whatever technique the therapist uses, the goal of Stage One—
hooking—must be kept uppermost in his mind. Stage One, accordingly, is not the place for confrontation or interpretation. It is not the
place to tear down social facades. Rather, it provides an occasion for
accentuating positive role behaviors and helping the participants feel
secure.

Bearing this in mind, the group therapist should take pains to
avoid embarrassing encounters in the early phases of treatment.
Wherever possible, group members should be forced to look at each
other's positive characteristics. This is especially important when
negative qualities are being heavily accentuated. This is seen in the
following episode taken from a family therapy.

> In an early therapy session during which the mother's role in the
> family was being explored, the remaining group members (the
> husband and two children) began to complain vehemently about
> her behavior. They spoke about her extrafamilial involvements
> (women's clubs, volunteer work, etc.), charging that she provided
> more comfort and solace to neighbors than she did to the family.
> This barrage continued for a while but was interrupted by the
> therapist by the simple comment: "But she must do some good
> things for you guys." After a brief hesitation, the husband con-
> fessed that she always made sure to have fresh shirts in his
> bureau drawer and that she was very good about keeping the
> house in order. The children followed suit by reluctantly admit-
> ting that their mother went out of her way to serve a different
> dessert at dinner every day.

These seemingly innocent admissions not only functioned to alter the
tone of the interactions but acted to reinstill the mother with some
confidence at a point in treatment where she was beginning to feel
incompetent and quite alone.

The end of a successful hooking stage occurs when each group
member feels quite positive about the group and the contribution he

is making to it. The shift from initial feelings of anxiety and distrust to feelings of safety and acceptance is behaviorally indexed by the tendency of individual members to rely upon the group as a source of comfort and advice. Comments that are common in this phase of treatment are:

"Knowing I can come here every week makes all the difference."

or

"Things don't seem so bad now that I'm able to share them."

Mullan and Rosenbaum (1962), commenting on the emergent group bond, write:

Early in group psychotherapy there is a strong feeling for "the group." Members often speak of "my group": "What will my group tell me to do?" "I wanted to bring it back to my group." ... All these expressions indicate a strong identification of each member with the group as an entity. (p. 61)

Mullan and Rosenbaum suggest that this identification derives from each group member's dual realization that he can be helped and can be of help to others. This of course is congruent with our observation, and it need only be added that the behavior accompanying this realization signals the completion of the first stage.

STAGE TWO: DE-ROLING

The second stage of group therapy represents the only completely novel stage in the treatment process. The rule of this stage entails a mild variety of social defrocking which, in its simplest form, involves prodding group members to relate in more direct ways. This is achieved by directing the members to tell each other what they are "really like." Although this typically involves some measure of self-revelation, de-roling does not approach the depth of self-disclosure reached later in treatment. In this phase of therapy, members are simply asked to go a bit beyond their facades, to relinquish some of their defensive postures, and to share parts of themselves which heretofore were glossed over or hidden from view.

Mullen and Rosenbaum, in their book *Group Therapy* (1962), comment on de-roling as it occurs in the early phases of the group:

Upon first entering the group [the members] are relatively conscious of their status, and are fixed in their roles; with time they
become more flexible, and finally they interact together, spontaneously assuming new and different roles. The new member
reacts to the others and to the therapist with a contrived role, the
one he has been taught to use, which enables him to cope with
others with a minimum of anxiety. This "role-taking" is discov-
ered in the therapy group and is discouraged. At first, this process arouses anxiety but eventually leads to a more realistic
attitude on the part of the new member. (p. 50)

They provide an example of this in the following excerpt:

Don was thirty years old and had been fired from a series of jobs
when he entered group therapy. He was most anxious to work in
"Wall Street," and showed an almost compulsive need to succeed by following the family pattern and goal of success "in the
Street." At his jobs he suppressed a tremendous anger and tried
to present a facade of compatibility, but his anger came through
the facade and he was fired again and again. Finally a personnel
supervisor in one of the brokerage houses where he was working
told him that arrogance was his problem. This sent Don into a
panic and a mood of despair. After a long interval, he obtained
another job "in the Street," but he became increasingly aware of
his inability to relate to his work with any comfort.
   It was then that he entered the group for psychotherapy. He
wore what he called "the uniform," the ultraconservative clothes,
and made a marked effort to emulate in attitude and speech his
concept of the "Wall Street broker." During his first session in
the group, Jimmy, another member from an environment as
status conscious and ordered as Don's, turned to Don and said,
"Open your vest and loosen up your collar. You don't have to
act here." (1962, p. 50)

As this example also indicates, it is not the therapist but another
group member who prompts the de-roling. We therefore are provided
with an instance of what earlier was referred to as "vesting." While in
the beginning of Stage Two it is the therapist who takes most of the
responsibility for de-roling, it is the group members who eventually
adopt this function. As the group moves in the direction of increasing

involvement, members who have de-roled will turn to members who have not and force them to follow suit.

An interesting de-roling technique, sometimes used in sensitivity groups, occurs in what might be called "I am" exercises. In such exercises, group members are required to make self-descriptive statements that progress from a level of superficiality to descriptions which strike at the core of their existence. An example observed in one encounter group, with a young woman as the subject, went as follows:

> I am . . . a teacher.
> I am . . . a college graduate.
> I am . . . a woman.
> I am . . . frustrated.
> I am . . . lonely.
> I am . . . desperate.

In traditional groups, movement toward deeper revelations usually occurs more slowly, although there is no real reason why exercises such as the foregoing could not be employed in any group.

One of the important byproducts of de-roling is that the therapy is converted from a "there-and-then" affair to one that is "here-and-now" in character. As group members divest themselves of the stereotyped behaviors associated with the roles of husband, wife, parent, executive, foreman, etc., they begin to focus more on immediate interchanges occurring in the group. As Stage Two draws to a close, the group members engage one another as intense, engaging, poignant human beings, not as sick story-tellers with pathetic tales of misery and woe. This is one of the indications that the stage is approaching completion.

Before leaving Stage Two, it might be mentioned that if questions of leadership arise, they typically arise at this point in the process. In group therapy, it is not uncommon to find the members challenging, confronting, and questioning the therapist's role as leader in the early phases of treatment. The issue that usually arises is whether the therapist should be allowed to remain in the role of a relatively detached participant-observer or whether he should "join" the group with equal status as group member. The therapist, as a result, often is asked to de-role, to join the group on a nonleader basis and share the inherent risks.

The therapist's response to this can be quite variable. Some leaders, believing that therapist and client should be on equal footing, share intimacies with the group; in the course of transactions involving trust and revelation, they engage in the same depth of self-exposure as the members do. Thus encounter group leaders sometimes divulge a great deal of personal information about themselves to their group (Nyberg, 1971), and some family therapists claim that they become a part of the family they are treating. It probably is safe to assume that a therapist's tendency to "enter" a group is based more on personal proclivities than on theoretical considerations.

There are a number of strong arguments that can be made *against* the therapist relinquishing his role as leader. Most group members, for one, feel safer with the therapist as leader rather than as co-member and, as indicated earlier, the creation of a secure milieu is an important consideration in the early stages of treatment. Secondly, a group without a leader has a tendency to meander, drift into tangents, and even disintegrate. Finally, even if the therapist vacates his role as leader, it never remains vacant for very long. Some group member invariably takes up the reins and leadership crises tend to crop up throughout the therapy, interfering in many instances with other, more important, matters.

There are, of course, groups in which a leadership crisis is deliberately precipitated (Bennis, 1964; Bion, 1959). In such groups, the therapy process includes a preliminary stage in which the leader refuses to meet certain of the group's demands. This usually causes a great deal of agitation and consternation and results in a direct challenge to the leader's position as organizer and director. The consequent resolution of this planned conflict then becomes a part of the therapeutic process. The stages which constitute this particular type of group obviously differ from interactional therapy as well as from most other forms of group therapy where leadership challenges are seen as extrinsic to, rather than an integral part of, the change process.

The resolution of whatever leadership issues arise and the successful execution of de-roling mark the end of this brief but important phase of group treatment. At the end of Stage Two, the group members have (1) moved from a position of role relating to one of more personal involvement and (2) begun to focus almost entirely on what is occurring in the here-and-now. Nevertheless the group members have not revealed anything that could truly be considered risky. They simply have gone a bit beyond the face they usually present to the world. But in so doing, they have set the stage for the appearance of maladaptive strategies.

STAGE THREE:
MALADAPTIVE STRATEGIES

By the time Stage Three is reached, the group has become a fairly tight-knit unit. The members have emerged somewhat from behind the social masks they wear and have begun to experience a sense of communal involvement. In this atmosphere of growing intimacy and vulnerability, certain interactional patterns begin to emerge, patterns that take the form of stereotyped social maneuvers. As Yalom (1970) puts it,

> ... given enough time, every patient will begin to be himself, to interact with the group members as he interacts with others in his social sphere, to create in the group the same interpersonal universe which he has always inhabited. In other words, patients will begin to display their maladaptive interpersonal behavior in the group; no need for them to describe their pathology—they will sooner or later act it out before the group's eyes. (p. 24)

As the members begin to perceive one another as potential sources of gratification, their idiosyncratic maladaptive strategies begin to emerge.

Specific strategies, be they dependency, martyr, sexuality, or any combination thereof, are manifested in one of two ways: in relation to particular group members, or in relation to the group at large. In the former case, strategies occur within specific pairings, while in the latter, they are manifested vis à vis the entire congregation. Instances of both are considered in the context of specific strategies.

Dependency strategies, when they occur in groups, are usually directed toward the group as a whole. When this happens, the dependent strategist communicates to the group that he depends upon it to make his life decisions for him. Through various devices, some subtle and some not so subtle, he lets it be known that if he is to continue to function, he must receive heavy doses of guidance and support. One way he does this is by continually dredging up for the group's consideration problems regarding relationships at work, decisions in school, and difficulties with family. Through such maneuvers, the dependent strategist adroitly casts himself in the role of "group ward."

The machinations of the dependent strategist become most apparent when he fails to solicit the support he seeks. When this occurs, the group then finds its time entirely taken up by the hostility and petulance of one frustrated member. In some instances, the group may be called upon to meet in an emergency session to solve a "crisis." This occurs when the strategist either decides he needs quick help with a crucial decision or when he communicates that he is fighting off suicidal impulses. The group, caught in the vise of collective guilt feelings, finds it difficult to refuse.

In some cases, the dependent strategist may focus on one member in the group who he believes can directly gratify his needs. When this happens, a pairing develops in which two members psychologically detach themselves from the group and form a "group" of their own. Both members of the resultant dyad subsequently attend to their own idiosyncratic needs and selfishly ignore everyone else. Bion, in *Experiences in Groups* (1959), traces this development to something he calls "a basic assumption of dependence." "Basic assumptions," according to Bion, are unconsciously derived, shared tendencies that underlie the growth of unhealthy liasions between group members. Although there are differences between Bion's theoretical premises and those contained in the interactional approach, the empirical referents, i.e., the interpersonal behaviors themselves, are identical.

Martyr strategies, like dependency strategies, also tend to be expressed primarily vis à vis the entire group, although they too may be expressed dyadically. Martyrs in groups can be recognized by their eagerness to offer themselves up as volunteers for nonverbal techniques, by their willingness to always take the first step in risky exchanges, and by their general willingness "to give." By sacrificing themselves for the greater good of the group, they take on the role of group guinea pig in the hope of exacting a toll of indebtedness from the other members.

Initial expressions of martyric behavior, whether in a traditional, family, or sensitivity group, often provide a source of amusement for the rest of the participants. The martyr makes sure that seats are properly arranged, busies himself filling the water pitcher, and makes sure all the ashtrays are clean. He offers to help the therapist set up his tape recorder, volunteers to run out for coffee, and is mindful to let the other members know when the session is over so that they are not late for other appointments. As the stage progresses and people are not particularly appreciative of his efforts, the martyr intensifies his efforts in order to gain the assurance that he so desperately needs. His behavior then is no longer comical but becomes painful and pathetic.

As in individual therapy, the efforts of the martyr strategist culminate in an overt demand for appreciation coupled with the implicit (and occasionally explicit) warning that the group will disintegrate without him. If his demands are not met, he may threaten to desert the group, a maneuver which succeeds if the group's concern leads it to implore him to remain for "the sake of the group." An alert therapist, as we will see in the next stage, prevents the group from capitulating, since this would testify to the strategy's success.

The use of sexuality strategies in groups recreates what is seen in individual therapy, the main difference being that the group members usually select each other as targets instead of the therapist. The precise patterns of strategic sexual behavior for males and females vary in the group just as they do in individual treatment: females tend toward physical demonstrativeness while males rely more on verbal devices.

Bion (1961), mentioned a moment ago in the context of dependency strategies, also notes the occurrence of sexual pairings in the group. Commenting on this phenomenon, he writes:

> Whenever two people begin to have this kind of relationship in the group—whether these two are a man and woman, man and man, or woman and woman—it seems to be a basic assumption, held both by the group and the pair concerned, that the relationship is a sexual one. ... If my observation of the group is correct, it is not suprising that ... an investigation (of dyads within the group) seems to demonstrate sex as occupying a central role. ... (pp. 61-63)

The topic of sex thus seems to play an important role in groups not merely as a topic of discussion but as an interactional phenomenon between group members.

The therapist's goal in Stage Three, whether we are speaking of dependency, martyr, or sexuality strategies, is to force an open and direct expression of the strategy. The goal is thus identical to that of the comparable stage in individual therapy, the salient difference once again being that the group replaces the therapist as the primary agent of change. To bring this about, all the therapist need do is redirect the thrust of confrontation and dare ploys so that the group members themselves do the forcing.

Thus, in the case of dependency strategies, the use of confrontation is expressed through statements such as:

"What is it you want the group to do for you?"

Remarks of this sort force the dependent strategist to make specific his vague assertions of helplessness and act to transform whatever he says from intra- to interpersonal types of communications.

In the martyr strategy, the generic forcing technique adopts the form of:

"How can the group show you its appreciation?"

Whenever the martyr sacrifices himself for the "good of the group" or acts with deference toward another member, the therapist either personally points up what he is doing or maneuvers the group so that specific members force the strategist to reveal what he expects in return for his help. Although at first the martyr may act indignant, professing deep hurt that his motives have been questioned, he usually will admit after continued prodding that all he wants in return is some acknowledgment of his usefulness. Further confrontation may even precipitate a threat to desert the group, a manipulation by which the martyr implicitly tries to raise the spectre of group disintegration.

The sexuality strategy is highlighted by focusing on the dyad in which the strategy is being employed and forcing the strategist to acknowledge what is going on between himself and his target. The forcing communication in this instance may take the form of:

"What would you do if you and (the target) were alone?"

or, more directly,

"Who in this group would you like to sleep with?"

As direct and blatant as the second remark seems, it is commonly relied upon in encounter groups to facilitate rapid exposure of sexuality strategies (Howard, 1970).

Exposing a sexual strategy, while admittedly a touchy subject, is not as difficult as it seems. Sexual strategists often couch their intents in fantasy terms such as dreams, and it is fairly simple to move from productions of this sort to relationships in the room. An example of this occurred in a group where one male client entertained the other group members on numerous occasions with detailed accounts of a sexual dream.

> The dream involved the exploits of a traveling salesman and included vivid seduction sequences in which the hero bedded down with more than one woman at a time. His strategic maneuver (arousal through titillation) was forced into the open by requiring the client to identify the women in his dreams. While at first he demurred ("Their faces are blurred"; "I can't make them out," etc.), he eventually admitted that they resembled two women in the group. While one of the women feigned disinterest, the other seemed fascinated by his exploits and asked him on occasion whether he had had any more such dreams. Following up on this led to exploration of the relationships "in the room."

Sexuality strategies, in short, must be forced into the open for the same reason other strategies are exposed—to establish the strategist's behavior as a manipulative interpersonal event.

While the examples offered in this section depict what takes place in cases where client strategies are well delineated, there are some clients for whom strategies are poorly developed or perhaps fused, as in the case of a sexuality-dependency strategy. Every member nevertheless should be expected to express in as direct a manner as possible what he truly wants from the group or from specific members. At the end of Stage Three, some form of strategic statement should have been made by every member of the group. Once this is accomplished, the stage is set for stripping.

STAGE FOUR: STRIPPING

The fourth stage of group therapy represents the fulcrum of the treatment process. Stripping, it will be recalled, entails refutation of the exposed strategy in the context of relational affirmation so as to render the strategy interpersonally dysfunctional. While in individual therapy this process was entirely in the hands of the therapist, in group therapy it is in the hands of the group. Since the group members are the targets of the strategy, they are the ones who must refute it.

The therapist's job is to help steer the group so that it does just this. Superficially, this seems to be an easy task. However, most group members do not readily take to turning away what seems to them simply to be an outstretched hand. After all, what harm is there in providing a little support for a "weak" member? What is lost in giving the group "mother" a nod of appreciation? What is really wrong in sleeping with someone who really cares for you? Nothing, really, in relationships marked by reciprocity. In relationships where strategies are operative, where mutuality is scarce or nonexistent, such moves are destined to fail. Playing the game by strategic rules only leads to the reinforcement and perseveration of strategic behavior.

Unfortunately, the potential victim has no way of knowing this beforehand; therefore, it is necessary for the therapist to appraise him of the dangers that lie ahead. This can be done by spelling out the consequences of strategic capitulation to individual members or to the group at large.

For example, if the group is asked to respond positively to the long-term commitment implicit in a dependent strategist's demands, the therapist might simply point out that a concession would require the group to remain together interminably. While an occasional member, usually another dependent strategist, may find this notion appealing, enough members will recognize the self-defeating consequences of such a commitment and will refute the strategic demand. In such cases, the strategist finds himself subjected to comments such as:

"We're tired of babying you every single session."

or

"It's time you stood on your own two feet."

Though comments of this sort are initially experienced as rejection, the bond that exists in the group tends to keep the dependent strategist from precipitously terminating.

The process of stripping can be observed in the following segment taken from a group therapy reported by Mullan and Rosenbaum (1962). In this excerpt, some of the group members are discussing the fact that one of them, Lana, left a previous session earlier than usual. The excerpt begins with the observation by one member that Lana told him she'd felt angry just before she left.

Fritzi: But you told me that you'd felt hostile.

> *Lana:* That, I always am. I felt I wasn't getting enough. I feel that way now. I'll be feeling that way the rest of my life.
>
> *Dennis:* So long, Lana . . .
>
> *Martha:* I thought you were very upset, and that's why you took off.
>
> *Therapist:* You said, "So long," Dennis. What do you mean?
>
> *Martha:* Dennis, don't you remember that you told Donald and me that you didn't trust Lana completely?
>
> *Dennis:* I don't trust her . . .
>
> *Martha:* Why?
>
> *Dennis:* I don't know.
>
> *Martha:* What is this feeling you have?
>
> *Dennis:* Well, I don't think it's important. It's probably part of my problem.
>
> *Martha:* That's why I'm asking.
>
> *Dennis:* Well, I said as long as I feel she's isolated herself, she's jumping out. You're gonna hang onto being demanding, you're gonna end up out in the cold in the Arctic Circle.
>
> *Fritzi (to Lana):* I think you're upset about the boyfriend you're going with, and you want us to help you with it, but you don't bring it in enough so we can help you.

Fritzi's comment regarding Lana's boyfriend momentarily takes the conversation "out of the room." Dennis, however, continues the stripping by telling Lana how he feels about her.

> *Dennis:* I ran out the door after you one night. I'll never do it again. You want a big play for sympathy. Well it's not enough either to get it or to give it. (p. 195)

Dennis' remarks, particularly his first and last in this excerpt, are salient examples of stripping responses. Turned off by what he correctly perceives as Lana's interpersonal manipulation, he responds in such a way as to refute her strategic demands.

The refutation-affirmation sequence in group therapy is obviously quite delicate and complex, skirting the thin line between acceptance and rejection. Nevertheless, the process must be repeated over and over until every member's strategic ways of relating are dealt with. This example of the pacing principle is an extended process which sometimes takes many months to complete, and it is not uncommon during this period to lose a member. It is therefore sometimes necessary to take unconventional steps to prevent premature terminations. In one group, for example, I physically prevented a female dependent strategist from fleeing the room in tears after she had been subjected to a stressful stripping episode. Blocking the door, I waited until she calmed down, after which the group took over and convinced her that they were not rejecting *her*, but rather her methods of manipulating them. She later confided that in the entire therapy this experience had been the most meaningful to her.

Perhaps the one important thing the therapist should remember is that stripping is always a traumatic experience. No matter how composed the client appears to be, he almost always experiences a tendency to flee. The therapist, being aware of this possibility, can therefore take precautions to prevent it.

Although the successful completion of the stripping stage marks an important turning point in the therapy, additional work still needs to be done. A behavioral vacuum has been created, and the participants must discover how to relate to one another in other than strategic ways. This search constitutes the major activity of Stage Five.

STAGE FIVE:
ADAPTIVE STRATEGIES

The appearance of risky revealing usually marks the beginning of Stage Five. The emotional impact associated with the refutation-affirmation experience of the previous stage predisposes group members to share parts of themselves never shared before. It is in this portion of therapy that strong feelings of incompetency, irresolvable difference, and worthlessness are brought up and openly discussed for the first time. The ability to engage in exchanges of this sort and to then profitably use the personal feedback which accompanies such transactions constitute a potent feature of group therapy.

The revealing process in Stage Five, once initiated, is taken over almost entirely by the membership. One by one the participants divulge their irrational wishes, strong fears, and shameful secrets; if anyone holds back, the group invariably sees to it that he "comes across." If there is one thing a group has an uncanny ability to detect, it is trivia being passed off as significant self-disclosures.

Some of the things revealed in groups are depicted in the following passages:

> A young married woman, who had entered therapy because she was frigid, reveals that she has lived for years with the suspicion that she has nymphomaniacal tendencies. Up until this point in treatment, her comments were restricted to complaints àbout marital problems.

> A young executive confesses that although smooth and self-assured in his business dealings, he feels insecure and incompetent. Fearing that he is nothing more than an empty shell, he tells the group that he has, in recent years, attempted suicide on two separate occasions.

> A middle-aged woman who entered therapy because of recurrent depressions tearfully confesses that her entire existence has been predicated on the assumption that her children desperately needed her. Now that they are going off to college she finds her very existence threatened.

Such revelations are not very different from those seen in individual treatment. The difference lies in the fact that in the group the client exposes himself to a variety of individuals, only one of whom is a professional. Although this obviously is a much more dangerous experience, it also has the potential for being much more rewarding. To know that others accept you as you are, regardless of your faults and failings, is one of the most significant experiences a human being can have.

Once risky revealing begins, it requires very little effort to get the feedback process rolling. Statements such as:

> *Th:* Jack has shared an important part of himself with us; perhaps we ought to share with him some of our feelings.

usually suffice. All the therapist need be wary of is the tendency for some members to respond to the risky revealing of others with pity or sympathy. Should this occur, it usually can be handled by pointing out to the group that they all can get someone to pat their head or pity them without too much difficulty and that they can be of more value to one another by supplying feedback. Most group members react positively to this and usually respond in the desired fashion.

Although the feedback rule functions in essentially the same manner in group therapy as individual treatment, there is a different emphasis. The main difference lies in the fact that the group contains greater potential for providing role feedback. Thus the group not only provides its individual members with feedback regarding personal characteristics such as facial expressions, vocal tone, body movements, etc., but offers feedback on how members react to one another as role surrogates. It is not uncommon in this phase of treatment therefore to hear individuals in the group preface their remarks with:

If I were married to you . . .

or

If I were one of your students . . .

or

I don't think I would enjoy working under you because . . .

or

As a woman . . .

Each member is thus afforded the opportunity to test out behaviors which beforehand were considered inappropriate or incompatible with the roles they played. The business executive, for example, may learn that a certain degree of closeness with subordinates does not necessarily vitiate authority or lead to disrespect. A husband may learn that being tender with his wife does not mean that he becomes less of a man in her eyes. Whenever people who fulfill complementary roles are found in a group, they provide valuable feedback of this sort for one another.

Although groups vary according to the types of role complementors contained within them (teachers-students; executives-workers; husbands-wives, etc.), practically every group contains members of both sexes. Most groups, therefore, can at the very least provide vital feedback for its members in the area of male-female relationships.

In the latter stages of a group therapy, a "love 'em and leave 'em" Don Juan confessed a deep fear of women and revealed that despite his callous behavior he was a very shy, sensitive person. The women in the group quickly picked up on this and told him that whereas earlier he had turned them off, they now felt very attracted to him as a man. The client was very surprised to learn that his heterosexual *saviour de faire* had been interpreted by them not as a desirable trait but as an indication that he regarded them as objects.

Experiences such as this provide important data for "re-roling," i.e., integrating role and intimacy behaviors so as to promote more effective interpersonal functioning.

Opportunities for role feedback abound in family therapy where complementary dyads such as husband-wife and parent-child are more the rule than the exception. This is illustrated in the following case study involving an adolescent boy and his parents. In this case, the identified patient, a fourteen-year-old only child, was being seen conjointly with his parents for difficulties that allegedly had to do with school problems.

Although the presenting problem had revolved about difficulties with peers and poor schoolwork, it later turned out that there were considerable problems at home. The boy was having difficulty relating to his father, although at times he seemed to go out of his way to model him. Nevertheless, there were numerous occasions in which the boy acted with hostility toward the father and often avoided him altogether. In one session during which the boy was pressed for an explanation for his behavior, he blurted out that being affectionate with his father would mean he was "a queer." The son had apparently equated tender feelings on his part as an indication of homosexuality. The father, shocked by his son's "confession," tried to convice him that this just wasn't so. The boy, nevertheless, refused to listen. I turned to the mother and asked her if she could tell her son what it was about her husband that made her feel like a woman. The mother then proceeded to tell the boy about his father's tenderness, his ability to cry in her presence, and the fact that he sought her out for support when he felt maligned by the world. The boy at first sat and listened to this in wide-eyed amazement but in a later session was able to talk about his love for his father. It was apparent from his subsequent behavior, moreover, that this episode had had a favorable impact on the family's interactions.

Feedback regarding intimacy and its integration with culturally pre-scribed role behaviors is, consequently, one of the unique features provided by the group experience.

The exchanges that occur in Stage Five ultimately result in the development of interpersonal behavior which could best be described as altruistic. The ability to extend oneself in the support of a person who fulfills a complementary role not only is the path to effective role functioning but underlies the development of selfish altruism. Recip-rocal roling, in short, is a mutually beneficial act, and its achievement is an important prerequisite for satisfying PnP. Stage Five ends then on a note of interpersonal reciprocity.

STAGE SIX:
UNHOOKING (TERMINATION)

The unhooking process that marks the final stage of group ther-apy differs quite a bit depending upon the type of group. In some groups, unhooking occurs spontaneously and with little effort, while in other groups it is more protracted and involved.* Whatever the case, the therapist takes a relatively passive stance in Stage Six unless, of course, certain members procrastinate. Under such circumstances he tends to prod the members in much the same way as he might in individual treatment.

Assuming, however, that the re-roling process described in Stage Five has been successfully negotiated, the members begin reorienting themselves to events in their "outside" lives. The emphasis on devel-oping adaptive social roles leads to a consideration of how one's experience in the group can be applied to relationships outside of it. Some individuals may have even begun applying what they have learned, so it is not unusual in this stage for members to come back to the group with stories of minor, although significant, successes:

A father, who had been having a great deal of difficulty relating to his teen-age son because of his tendency to always make his son (and people generally) commit themselves first in a relation-

*Specific differences are discussed later under the headings of Family and Sensi-tivity Groups.

ship, proudly told the group: "I told my son that *I wanted to go* camping with him and his face lit up like a Christmas tree."

A female member with marital problems, who had refused to do even simple things for her husband because she felt it signified submission on her part, reported: "I made a picnic lunch and met him at the office. We spent his lunch hour in the park. He was flabbergasted; it was just like we were on a date."

In both instances, we see the client commit himself in a relationship by means of a nonconditional affirmative act. Though such acts may seem small and insignificant to outsiders, they assume a great deal of meaning in troubled relationships.

Not all attempts at establishing productive relationships occur this smoothly. Sometimes, interpersonal growth means terminating a low payoff relationship in order to clear the way for a more productive one:

A woman in a marital-problems group (singles who were separated or divorced) told the group that she had finally left her "ex-husband" as a result of her experiences in the group. Though the two had been divorced for many months, her dependent ties led her to devise and perpetuate an arrangement in which her ex-husband would come over every night for dinner and sleep with her on a weekly or bi-weekly basis. Attempts to establish other relationships during this period remained at a standstill for both. The client's ability to relate to members of the group in other than dependent ways led her to terminate this arrangement so that both she and her ex-husband could go their separate ways.

The conditions under which interpersonal growth occurs is obviously a function of each member's unique life circumstances.

The group's movement from discussion of here-and-now interactions to discussion of relationships outside the group signifies that the treatment process is nearing its end. As relationships in the outside world become more fruitful and satisfactory, relationships within the group begin to decrease in significance. The husbands, wives, students, and co-workers who are the significant figures for the group members and who are capable of providing long-term payoffs are not within the small group but in the larger society. As this realization develops, the therapy comes to a close.

The group process that has been described in the previous pages is an obvious extrapolation of the stages and rules described in Chapter Four. And just as the individual process is thought to be generalizable, so the group process is thought to have a generic base. This is why examples from traditional groups, family therapy, and T-groups were used in describing the various stages of the group process. Gendlin and Beebe, writing on experiential groups, echo this sentiment:

> A powerful group process is being discovered and used under different names in different settings. Some of its names are sensitivity group, T-group, brain-storming, creativity group, encounter group, development group, group psychotherapy, marathon group. Some of its settings are schools, churches, industry, campus politics, hospitals, consulting offices, private homes.
>
> The different approaches and settings involve the same experiential process ... Differences in words and roles must not obscure the fact that in each instance, the individuals are seeking one and the same process, variously called "seeking to overcome alienation," "seeking to be more alive in roles and words," and (to make the roles and words stretch to permit this) "seeking to be more open, more in touch with what they like and feel," "more expressive," "more spontaneous," "more real and genuine," "more honest with themselves and others," and "more in the world rather than silent, dumb, isolated, and frozen in mere empty role-playing." Note that each of these phrases refers to the same concrete process occurring in an individual, even though these phrases stem from different fields and verbal contexts and are at home in quite different social settings. The manner of verbal and institutional behavior is changing from alienation to experientially interactive. (1968, p. 191-192)

Although Gendlin's focus is on the experiencing process, his use of the term "experientially interactive" makes it probable that what he describes bears a great deal of similarity to what has been described in the preceding pages.

Although the process is thought to be generic, structural differences still exist among various types of groups. The remainder of this chapter, therefore, is devoted to an examination of family and sensitivity groups in an effort to uncover precisely how they differ from more traditional approaches to group change.

FAMILY THERAPY

Treatment of the family as a group is based on the dual assumptions that (1) the family constitutes a behavioral system in its own right and (2) disturbances in individual family members can be traced to disturbances in the system (Ackerman, 1972). From a structural, or process, perspective, the fact that the family constitutes a pre-existing system, i.e., is made up of prior role relationships, is reflected most saliently in the latter stages of treatment. There are, however, other changes that derive from this consideration. We therefore consider the various stages of family therapy in sequence.

Very little need be said about the first, or hooking, stage of family therapy, except to note that it does not decrease in significance simply because a family is being seen. The beginning therapist should not assume that all the members of a family are uniformly motivated merely because they enter treatment as a unit. In many cases the child is in the consulting room not because he wants to be but because he is forced to be. The same sometimes holds true for one, or both, parents. Most parents arrive at the clinic with "a disturbed child," and though they may be persuaded that family treatment is the treatment of choice, they often remain skeptical and resistant.

For these reasons, it is always necessary to invoke hooking procedures with all families and with all family members. This sometimes necessitates a delicate juggling act, requiring the therapist to take the parents' side in one instance and the child's in the next. It is not uncommon, therefore, to find the therapist directing statements of the following sort to the parents:

> "It must be frustrating to have to keep telling Jimmy things over and over and find it's like talking to the wall."

and to say to the child in the same session:

> "No matter how hard you try, you don't seem to be able to satisfy your folks."

If the therapist neglects to engage in emotional coupling with *all* the family members, he may find later in treatment that father begins missing sessions because he suddenly has to work late, or that Johnny has an upset stomach and has to stay in bed. Consequently, it is better to always engage in hooking when working with families rather than assume that strong pervasive family motivation for treatment exists.

Stage Two is perhaps the first place where the influence of pre-existing role relationships is felt. De-roling, it will be remembered, involves relinquishing certain stereotyped facades in the service of greater intimacy and involvement. In groups made up of strangers, the difficulties in accomplishing this are not excessive, since whatever occurs within the group tends to be group-specific. The business executive who reveals certain self-doubts and insecurities about himself does so in the knowledge that his "secrets" will be kept inside the group. He need not worry that outsiders such as his subordinates will find out things about him that he does not want them to know. In other words, there is a distinct "inside" and "outside" group in traditional group therapy.

In contrast, there is no inside-outside distinction in family therapy: the "inside" group *is* the "outside" group. Whatever a family member does in the therapy session has immediate and direct implications for the ways he or she is regarded in the day-to-day interactions of the family (Bell, 1972, p. 141). A father who momentarily steps outside his usual authoritarian role, for example, has to face the implications of such a move for his functioning as family disciplinarian. Although such a move may prove beneficial in the long run, it can be very threatening in the early stages of treatment.

For these reasons, it is necessary that the second stage of family therapy be conducted in a careful and deliberate manner. This does not require any changes in the de-roling process, per se, but simply entails balancing the amount and extent of self-disclosure. The pacing principle must, in other words, be stringently adhered to in order to prevent individual family members from becoming too vulnerable too early. If there is one major quantitative procedural shift in family therapy, it is the time spent conducting de-roling in the second stage of treatment.

Generally speaking, Stages Three, Four, and Five follow the interactional process outlined earlier. Because of the greater emphasis on de-roling in Stage Two, it is sometimes necessary to spend a greater amount of time in Stage Five discussing "re-roling." This, however, is a quantitative rather than a qualitative difference and thus involves no changes in the rules or tactics of this stage.

One tactical change that needs to be considered, however, is the question of how to handle sexuality strategies, particularly when they tend to characterize the relationship of parent and child. While not a common strategy in families, sexuality strategies are often seen in very disturbed or schizophrenic families. In such instances, the pattern is usually one of fairly blatant seductivity between mother and child.

The issue of parent-child sexuality is obviously a highly charged one and if handled poorly can result in a precipitous termination. For this reason, forcing and confronting such strategies should be avoided by beginning therapists. An alternative is to bypass exploration of the relationship itself and to focus instead on how the two people involved might develop more independent activities. Often this acts to defuse the strategy by indirectly toning down its intensity.

When a sexuality strategy dominates the *parental dyad*, however, the therapist may wish to attack it directly by isolating the parents and continuing the treatment as a marital therapy. This is often done even when a sexuality strategy is not the issue, the assumption being that improved marital interactions will be reflected in improved parent-child relationships. However, once the decision is made to exclude the children, it is difficult to re-integrate them in the therapy at a later time.

Finally, it should be noted that children can be as manipulative as adults in their interpersonal dealings. While young children often do not have well-developed strategies, they are nonetheless quite adept at controlling their parents via poor school performance, playing one parent against the other, and so on. Although children are indisputably manipulated by their parents, the beginning therapist must realize that this is a two-way street and that the "helpless" child is rarely as helpless as he seems.

The major difference between family and traditional group therapy occurs at the end of the treatment process. Since there is no "inside-outside" distinction in family therapy, the generalization function of Stage Six becomes superfluous. As a consequence, family therapy terminates when adaptive strategies start to characterize the group's interactions. Stage Five, in other words, becomes the last stage in the treatment process in family therapy.

The family therapy process, in sum, does not deviate greatly from the generic group process outlined earlier. There are some differences with regard to the time and energy invested in particular stages, but the sequencing of stages remains essentially the same. The primary difference lies in the omission of Stage Six. In family therapy, completion of the treatment process is for all intents and purposes synonymous with the completion of Stage Five. Once the family has begun to interact in adaptive ways, risking themselves with one another and supplying each other with pertinent feedback, the therapy can be terminated.

In the systems we consider next, sensitivity groups, more drastic changes take place. Not only are certain stages omitted, but the character of the remaining stages is often markedly altered. The result is a change process which departs significantly from those already described.

SENSITIVITY GROUPS

The use of small groups to achieve personal and/or organizational growth is an integral part of what is often referred to as the Human Potential Movement. This "movement" springs from two dominant influences—the Esalen Institute headquartered at Big Sur, California, and NTL (National Training Laboratories) based in Bethel, Maine.

At Esalen the emphasis is on producing *personal change* by promoting self and interpersonal awareness. With roots in Gestalt therapy, Esalen relies upon physical and sensory experiences such as dance and massage and on unique kinds of social interactions to achieve its goals. These interactions occur in gatherings called Encounter groups in which participants are forced to confront each other as a means of learning how they affect others and how others affect them (Egan, 1970; Schutz, 1967).

The NTL approach, with roots in Lewinian field theory, focuses more on *organizational change.* To achieve their goals, NTL leaders (facilitators, trainers) conduct workshops, or "laboratories," in which the focus is on authority and leadership issues, communication processes, and the dynamics of group change. Much of the learning involved in these laboratories takes place in small group interactions referred to as T-groups ("T" for training). Although differences exist, much of what happens in T-groups bears a great deal of similarity to what takes place in Encounter groups (Lakin, 1972, Ch. 1).

Both Encounter and T-groups are designed to promote healthier human relationships by encouraging more honest and direct communication. This is accomplished by delving into current feelings and reactions and by exploring the ways in which members verbally and nonverbally influence one another. The goal is to sensitize people to their own reactions—hence the term "sensitivity" to describe groups in which the major emphasis is on (1) learning interpersonal skills and (2) using the temporal and spacial reality of the group as the learning medium(Egan, 1970, p. 5).

It is perhaps apparent that these criteria do not fully differentiate sensitivity groups from other types of groups. In both group and family therapy, the therapist also concentrates on interpersonal maneuvers as they occur in a here-and-now context. What, then, distinguishes sensitivity groups from more traditional groups? The answer lies in their unique format. Specifically, it is the time frame of sensitivity groups that sets them apart from other group endeavors. Most sensitivity groups are designed to begin and finish what they have to do in a matter of days rather than months or years. A listing of the types of offerings at some of the more well-known human potential centers (Bethel, Esalen, Kairos, etc.) reveals that many of their groups last only about a week or two, with most lasting only a weekend. It is this—the notion of *accelerated change*—that provides some clue to the nature of process changes in sensitivity groups.

The fact that sensitivity groups must accomplish their goals in a short period of time affects the group process in two ways. First, several of the stages are almost completely eliminated, existing as vestigial remnants if at all. Secondly, the activities in the remaining stages are greatly condensed to fit into the available time. The result is an abbreviated change process, one which allows the maximum use of resources in the shortest possible time.

The most immediate consequence of accelerated change is the elimination of standard hooking procedures. Since the format of short-term groups does not lend itself to an extended preparatory phase, Stage One is essentially done away with and certain extratherapeutic factors are relied upon instead to provide the stick-to-it-iveness which hooking is meant to achieve. One of these factors is the implicit, and often explicit, hope which sensitivity groups hold out for their participants. The advertisements and even the technical literature in this area are replete with veiled promises of self-fulfillment, personal growth, or peak experiences. Another factor is the economic commitment that participants make; advance payments ranging from $50 to $150 usually generate enough motivation to help members withstand for brief periods of time what many would consider to be harrowing experiences. Finally, massive doses of support are provided throughout the group process to carry the participants through the turmoil of intense, short-term change.

The elimination of Stage One makes Stage Two, or de-roling, the initial stage in sensitivity groups. But since there is limited time available, de-roling must be conducted in an abridged fashion. One of the ways this is done is by requiring participants to leave their usual social surroundings and to sleep, eat, and live at the site of the encounter or laboratory. As members leave their normal environments, the societal props that reinforce the different social roles they play are typically left behind.

Instant de-roling is sometimes also accomplished by requiring participants to temporarily adopt new identities. Some sensitivity groups ask their members to take new names, cautioning them not to reveal what they do or from where they come. The directness with which people engage one another when "Where do you come from?" and "What do you do for a living?" are removed from their behavioral repetoires is often quite revealing.

A dramatic instance of de-roling occurs in nude therapy, where doffing one's clothing acts as a prerequisite for further interactions. Although the sensational aspects of nude therapy has caught the fancy of the mass media and the public, nudity per se is not particularly therapeutic. The willinginess of group members to remove their clothes in front of one another, however, functions as a symbolic indication of a willingness to go beyond surface presentations. As a preliminary group maneuver, nudity can, under certain circumstances, therefore act to facilitate the de-roling process.

Regardless of how de-roling is accomplished, once it is completed the group quickly moves into the succeeding stages. Stages Three, Four, and Five, as usual, are addressed to the essentials of the interpersonal change process, dealing with issues of closeness, self-disclosure, and interpersonal risk-taking. But once again, the issue of time has to be taken into account. The problem, briefly stated, is: how does one move the group from an interpersonal stance of guardedness and social duplicity toward one that is open, honest, and dyadically productive—in a brief period of time?

The answer lies in the use of therapeutic maneuvers referred to as nonverbal techniques. Techniques of this sort revolve about physical exercises designed to highlight issues of trust, dependency, and interpersonal acceptance. One such exercise requires a single member to stand with his back to another and let himself freely fall into the other's arms; the issue of trust then often arises as the participants discuss their feelings prior to, during, and after their fall. Another nonverbal technique, called "break-in," requires one member to try to enter a human ring formed by the remaining members; this usually leads to a rather intense emotional reaction and the sharing of feelings regarding acceptance and rejection. A variety of nonverbal techniques are described by Schutz in *Joy* (1967) as well as in manuals published by others working in the area (Watson, 1967; Pfeiffer & Jones, 1969).

The rationale underlying the use of "nonverbals" centers in the belief that strong emotional feelings are capable of being expressed more directly through physical channels than through words. Based on the observation that interpersonal defenses are largely verbal in nature, such techniques attempt to circumvent these defenses by forcing interactions through nonverbal channels. Attempts to engage in lengthy intellectual inquiries and explanations, referred to as "mind-fucking" in some circles, are viewed with suspicion in sensitivity groups and are bypassed in favor of exercises involving body movement and touch.

The acceleration of the change process in sensitivity groups does not substantially alter any of the rules contained in Stages Three, Four, and Five. It does, however, create a situation wherein the rules of these stages overlap one another. Since Stages Three, Four, and Five are sometimes telescoped, their techniques paradoxically occur in different sequence than they would ordinarily. Thus, affirmation, which in traditional groups precedes risky revealing, usually follows it in sensitivity groups. By applying group pressure to "let it all hang out," the leader forces individual members to divulge personal data without waiting for close relationships to develop. The apprehension this often generates is consequently handled by intense demonstrations of affection and support such as hugging, kissing, and rocking. The normal "affirmation-revealing" sequence is thus inverted in sensitivity groups in the service of accelerated change.

Although the telescoping of the rules in the interior stages of the process and the speed with which change occurs sometimes make it difficult to observe the operation of maladaptive strategies, they nevertheless constitute the focus in sensitivity groups. This is demonstrated in the following statement by a woman who was a participant in an encounter group:

> All my life I felt that I couldn't really compete with other women, because of my body. So, instead, I became a "helper"— thus I was not a threat to them and they liked and accepted me. It worked the same way with men. I could never be thought of as a woman, to be desired physically, so I became a mother to the men. The helper role was genuine sometimes, but too often it was just a role, so that they would accept me, but on "safe" ground— always intellectual, never physical. The helper role had become so integrated into my personality that I couldn't distinguish any longer between really wanting to help or using it as a hiding device. (Schutz, 1967, pp. 106-107)

This example of a martyr strategy also provides some insight as to the way short-term interpersonal solutions grow into highly ingrained social styles.

The completion of Stage Five in most sensitivity groups marks the end of the group process. Since time does not allow for extensive postmortems, Stage Six is entirely eliminated. This perhaps explains why many participants report that their experiences in such groups have only a marginal and fleeting impact on subsequent interactions. Since the generalization stage is neglected, participants have little opportunity to transfer what they have learned to their back-home existence (Cashdan, 1970).

The process underlying sensitivity groups, in short, can be theoretically depicted as an abbreviated and truncated version of the six-stage change process described in the initial portions of this chapter. Stages One and Six are completely omitted, with the remaining stages condensed so as to produce change in as expedient a manner as possible. It is this factor that structurally distinguishes sensitivity groups from more traditional approaches to behavior change.*

---

* Some workers contend that the major difference between sensitivity and traditional groups lies in the nature of their clientele. Sensitivity groups, they maintain, are designed to deal with normals, while traditional groups treat "sick" persons. Whatever merit is possessed by this "therapy for normals" position, it does not differentiate

Both family and sensitivity groups represent variations on the generic group theme presented earlier. Still, it is necessary to keep in mind that the distinctions made in this chapter are not hard and fast. Innovations abound in the group area, sometimes creating more chaos than clarity. Some of the confusion can be avoided, however, if one focuses not so much on manifest techniques but on the process that underlies them. A close look at Marathon groups, for example, reveals that they are more akin to sensitivity groups than they are to traditional therapy groups (Mintz, 1971; Stoller, 1968). Since both involve accelerated change, they must lay claim to processes which are practically identical. In a similar vein, T-groups involving members of a single business organization or school system often resemble family therapy more than sensitivity groups, since both are comprised of members who possess pre-existing role relationships. Such T-groups, in fact, are even referred to in the literature as "family groups." Attending to the process, in sum, enables one to comprehend more subtle changes that take place on the level of technique.

SUMMARY AND CONCLUSIONS

The material presented in this chapter documents some of the critical processes involved in group psychotherapy. Relying upon principles of strategic change, I have tried to show how the therapist guides the group in such a direction so as to facilitate individual growth. The differences between group and individual treatment were highlighted, as were some of the procedural differences among various types of groups. A basic assumption throughout the chapter was that traditional, family, and sensitivity groups converge along interactional lines so that their similarities outweigh their differences.

The basic purpose of this book has been to call attention to the nature of process in psychotherapy. Toward this end, developmental sequences for several forms of psychotherapy were constructed to show how stages and rules generate therapeutic technique. My ultimate goal was to articulate as systematically as possible the technical aspects of psychotherapy without vitiating the fundamental human character of the encounter. To the extent that the reader is able to use this knowledge to increase his therapeutic effectiveness, this goal will have been realized.

---

groups along structural lines but merely points up differences that may exist in initial screening procedures.

BIBLIOGRAPHY

Ackerman, N.W. *Treating the troubled family.* New York: Basic Books, 1966.

Ackerman, N.W. Family psychotherapy—theory and practice. In G.D. Erickson and T.P. Hogan (Eds.), *Family therapy: An introduction to theory and technique.* Belmont, California: Wadsworth, 1972.

Alexander, F. and French, T.M. *Psychoanalytic therapy.* New York: Ronald Press, 1946.

Bell, J.E. *Family group therapy.* Public Health Monograph No. 64. Washington, D.C.: U.S. Government Printing Office, 1961.

Bell, J.E. A theoretical position for family group therapy. In G.D. Erickson and T.P. Hogan (Eds.), *Family therapy: An introduction to theory and technique.* Belmont, California: Wadsworth, 1972.

Bellak, L. and Small, L. *Emergency psychotherapy and brief psychotherapy.* New York: Grune & Stratton, 1965.

Bennis, W.G. Patterns and vicissitudes in T-group development. In L.P. Bradford, J.R. Gibbs, and K.D. Benne (Eds.), *T-group theory and laboratory method.* New York: Wiley, 1964.

Bergin, A.E. The evaluation of therapeutic outcomes. In A.E. Bergin and S.L. Garfield (Eds.), *Handbook of psychotherapy and behavior change.* New York: Wiley, 1971.

Berne, E. *The structure and dynamics of organizations and groups.* New York: Lippincott, 1963.

Berne, E. *Games people play: The psychology of human relationships.* New York: Grove Press, 1964.

Bion, W. *Experiences in groups.* New York: Basic Books, 1959.

Blumer, H. *Symbolic interactionism.* New York: Prentice-Hall, 1969.

Bordin, E.S. Inside the therapeutic hour. In E.A. Rubinstein and M.B. Parloff (Eds.), *Research in psychotherapy.* Washington, D.C.: American Psychological Association, 1959.

Bradford. L.P., Gibb, J.R., and Benne, K.D. (Eds.) *T-group theory and laboratory method.* New York: Wiley, 1964.

Cameron, N. and Magaret, A. *Behavior pathology.* Boston: Houghton-Mifflin, 1951.

Caplan, G. *Principles of preventive psychiatry.* New York: Basic Books, 1964.

Carson, R.C. *Interaction concepts of personality.* Chicago: Aldine, 1969.

Cashdan, S. Delusional thinking and the induction process in schizophrenia. *Journal of Consulting Psychology,* 1966, **30**, 207-212.

Cashdan, S. The use of drawings in child psychotherapy: A process analysis of a case study. *Psychotherapy: Theory, Research and Practice,* 1967, **4** (2), 81-86.

Cashdan, S. Sensitivity groups—Problems and promise. *Professional Psychology,* 1970, Spring, 217-224.

Cashdan, S. *Abnormal psychology.* Englewood Cliffs, New Jersey: Prentice-Hall, 1972.

Egan, G. *Encounter: Group processes for interpersonal growth.* Belmont, California: Brooks-Cole, 1970.

Ellis, A. *Reason and emotion in psychotherapy.* New York: Lyle Stuart, 1962.

Fenichel, O. Brief psychotherapy. In H. Fenichel and D. Rapaport (Eds.), *The collected papers of Otto Fenichel.* New York: Norton, 1954.

Ford, D.H. and Urban, H.B. *Systems of psychotherapy.* New York: Wiley, 1963.

Foulkes, S.H. and Anthony, E.J. *Group psychotherapy.* London: Penguin Books, 1957.

Fromm-Reichman, F. *Principles of intensive psychotherapy.* Chicago: University of Chicago Press, 1950.

Garfield, S.L. and Kurz, M. Evaluation of treatment and related procedures in 1,216 cases referred to a mental hygiene clinic. *Psychiatric Quarterly,* 1952, **25,** 414-424.

Gendlin, E. and Beebe, J. Experiential groups. In G. Gazda (Ed.), *Innovations in group psychotherapy.* Springfield, Illinois: Charles C Thomas, 1968.

Goffman, E. On cooling the mark out: Some aspects of adaptation to failure. In W.G. Bennis, E.H. Schein, E.I. Steele, and D.E. Berlew (Eds.), *Interpersonal dynamics.* Homewood, Illinois: Dorsey, 1968.

Goffman, E. *Relations in public: Microstudies of the public order.* New York: Basic Books, 1971.

Goldstein, A.P., Heller, K., and Sechrest, L.B. *Psychotherapy and the psychology of behavior change.* New York: Wiley, 1966.

Gouldner, A.W. The norm of reciprocity: A preliminary statement. *American Sociological Review,* 1960, **25,** 161-178.

Greenburg, D. *How to be a Jewish mother.* Los Angeles: Price, Stern and Sloan, 1964.

Greenson, R. *The technique and practice of psychoanalysis. I.* New York: International Universities Press, 1967.

Haley, J. *Strategies of psychotherapy.* New York: Grune & Stratton, 1963.

Harlow, H.F., Harlow, M.K., and Suomi, S.J. From thought to therapy: Lessons from a primate laboratory. *American Scientist,* 1971, **59,** 538-549.

Heron, W. Cognitive and physiological effects of perceptual isolation. In M.D. Solomon, P.E. Kubzansky, P.H. Leiderman, J.H. Mendelson, R. Trumbull, and D. Wexler (Eds.), *Sensory deprivation.* Cambridge, Massachusetts: Harvard University Press, 1961.

Hobbs, N. Group-centered psychotherapy. In C. Rogers (Ed.), *Client-centered therapy.* Boston: Houghton-Mifflin, 1951.

Homans, G. Social behavior as exchange. *American Journal of Sociology,* 1958, **63,** 597-606.

Homans, G. *Social behavior: Its elementary forms.* New York: Harcourt, Brace & World, 1961.

Howard, J. *Please touch.* New York: McGraw-Hill, 1970.

Jackson, D. and Weakland, J. Conjoint family therapy: Some considerations on theory, technique and results. *Psychiatry,* 1961, **24,** 30-45.

Jackson, D.D. Family rules. *Archives of General Psychiatry,* 1965, **12,** 589-594.

Jourard, S.M. *The transparent self.* Princeton, New Jersey: Van Nostrand, 1964.

Kiesler, D.J. Experimental designs in psychotherapy research. In A.E. Bergin and S.L. Garfield (Eds.), *Handbook of psychotherapy and behavior change.* New York: Wiley, 1971.

Klein, D. and Lindemann, E. Preventive intervention in individual and family crisis situations. In G. Caplan (Ed.), *Prevention of mental disorders in children.* New York: Basic Books, 1961.

Lakin, M. *Interpersonal encounter: Theory and practice in sensitivity training.* New York: McGraw-Hill, 1972.

Lang, P.J. Experimental studies in desensitization psychotherapy. In J. Wolpe, A. Salter, and L.J. Reyna (Eds.), *The conditioning therapies.* New York: Holt, Rinehart & Winston, 1964.

Leary, T. *Interpersonal diagnosis of personality.* New York: Ronald Press, 1957.

Lennard, H.L. and Bernstein, A. *Patterns in human interaction.* San Francisco: Jossey-Bass, 1969.

Lennard, H.L., Epstein, L.J., Bernstein, A., and Ransom, D.C. *Mystification and drug misuse.* New York: Harper & Row (Perennial Library), 1971.

Levy, L.H. Fact and choice in counseling and counselor education: A cognitive viewpoint. Paper presented at Counselor Education Seminar, University of Minnesota, 1967.

Lewin, K.K. *Brief psychotherapy.* St. Louis: Green, 1970.

Lindesmith, A.R. and Strauss, A. *Social psychology.* New York: Holt, Rinehart & Winston, 1968.

London, P. *The modes and morals of psychotherapy.* New York: Holt, Rinehart & Winston, 1964.

Matarazzo, J. D. Psychotherapeutic processes. In P.R. Farnsworth, O. McNemar, and Q. McNemar (Eds.), *Annual review of psychology.* Palo Alto, California: Annual Review, Inc., 1965, **16,** 181-224.

Matarazzo, J.D. The practice of psychotherapy is an art and not a science. In A.R. Maher and L. Pearson (Eds.), *Creative developments in psychotherapy.* Cleveland: Case Western Reserve Press, 1971.

Menninger, K. *Theory of psychoanalytic technique.* New York: Basic Books, 1958.

Mensh, I.N. and Golden, J.M. Factors in psychotherapeutic success. *Journal of Missouri Medical Association.* 1951, **48,** 180-184.

Mintz, E.E. *Marathon groups.* New York: Appleton, 1971.

Muench, G.A. An investigation of the efficacy of time-limited psychotherapy. *Journal of Counseling Psychology,* 1965, **12,** 294-298.

Mullan, H. and Rosenbaum, M. *Group psychotherapy.* New York: Free Press, 1962.

Nemeth, C. A critical analysis of research utilizing the prisoner's dilemma paradigm for the study of bargaining. In L. Berkowitz (Ed.), *Advances in experimental social psychology.* New York: Academic Press, 1972.

Nyberg, D. One small-group leader's paradoxical problems of becoming a member of his own group. In G. Egan (Ed.), *Encounter groups: Basic readings.* Belmont, California: Brooks-Cole, 1971.

Pfeiffer, J.W. and Jones, J.E. *Structured experiences for human relations training.* Iowa City: University Associates Press, 1969.

Pratt, J.H. The home sanitarium treatment of consumption. *Johns Hopkins Hospital Bulletin,* 1906, **17,** 140-144.

Rabkin, R. *Inner and outer space.* New York: Norton, 1970.

Rogers, C. A process conception of psychotherapy. *American Psychologist,* 1958, **13,** 141-149.

Rogers, C. A theory of therapy, personality, and interpersonal relationships as developed in the client-centered framework. In S. Koch (Ed.), *Psychology: A study of a science. III. Formulations of the person and the social context.* New York: McGraw-Hill, 1959.

Rogers, C. A process conception of psychotherapy. In *On becoming a person.* Boston: Houghton-Mifflin, 1961.

Rokeach, M. *The three Christs of Ypsilanti.* New York: Knopf (Vintage Books), 1964.

Ruitenbeek, H.M. *The new group therapies.* New York: Discus, 1970.

Satir, V. *Conjoint family therapy.* Palo Alto, California: Science and Behavior Books, 1967.

Schutz, W. *Joy.* New York: Grove Press, 1967.

Shepard, M. *The love treatment.* New York: Paperback Library, 1971.

Schlien, J.M., Mosak, H.H., and Dreikers, R. Effects of time limits: A comparison of two psychotherapies. *Journal of Counseling Psychology,* 1962, **9,** 31-34.

Small, L. *The briefer psychotherapies.* New York: Brunner-Mazel, 1971.

Stampfl, T.G. and Levis, D.J. Essentials of implosive therapy: A learning-theory-based psychodynamic behavioral therapy. *Journal of Abnormal and Social Psychology,* 1967, **72,** 496-503.

Stoller, F.H. Marathon group therapy. In G.M. Gazda (Ed.), *Innovations to group therapy.* Springfield, Illinois: Charles C Thomas, 1968.

Stone, G.P. and Farberman, H.A. (Eds.) *Social psychology through symbolic interaction.* Waltham, Massachusetts: Ginn-Blaisdell, 1970.

Strupp, H.H. and Bergin, A.E. Some empirical and conceptual bases for coordinated research in psychotherapy: A critical review of issues, trends, and evidence. *International Journal of Psychiatry,* 1969, **7**, 18-90.

Sullivan, H.S. *The interpersonal theory of psychiatry.* New York: Norton, 1953.

Sullivan, H.S. *The psychiatric interview.* New York: Norton, 1970. Originally published by William Alanson White Psychiatric Foundation, 1954.

Thibaut, J.W. and Kelley, H.H. *The social psychology of groups.* New York: Wiley, 1959.

Watson, G. *Exercises for laboratory training.* Union, New Jersey: Laboratory for Applied Behavioral Science, 1967.

Watzlawick, P., Beavin, J.H., and Jackson, D.D. *Pragmatics of human communication.* New York: Norton, 1967.

Wolberg, L.R. *Short-term psychotherapy.* New York: Grune & Stratton, 1965.

Wolf, A. and Schwartz, E.K. *Psychoanalysis in groups.* New York: Grune & Stratton, 1962.

Wolpe, J. *Psychotherapy by reciprocal inhibition.* Stanford, California: Stanford University Press, 1958.

Wolpe, J. *The practice of behavior therapy.* New York: Pergamon, 1969.

Yalom, I. *The theory and practice of group psychotherapy.* New York: Basic Books, 1970.

Index

Ackerman, N. W., 103, 129
Adaptive Strategies stage
  in family therapy, 130-131
  in group therapy, 122-126
  in individual therapy, 63, 91-97
  in sensitivity groups, 134, 135
Advising, 65
  technique of, 68-70
Alexander, F., and T. M. French, 5
Analysis stage, of brief
  psychotherapy, 39
Anthony, E. J., and S. H. Foulkes,
  103
Anxiety
  systematic desensitization and, 31-
  33
  treatment of, 7

Beavin, J. H., D. D. Jackson, and P.
  Watzlawick, 49-50
Beebe, J., and E. Gendlin, 128
Behavior change, psychotherapy
  and, 1-2

Behavior therapy, process of, 31-36
Bell, J. E., 103, 130
Bellak, L., and L. Small, 38
Bennis, W. G., 114
Bergin, A. E., 11
Bergin, A. E., and H. H. Strupp, 11
Berne, E., 42, 52, 103
Bion, W., 114
Blumer, H., 42, 44
Bordin, E., 100
Bradford, L. P., 103
Brief psychotherapy technique, 36-38
Briefer Psychotherapies, The (Small),
  37

Cameron, N., and A. Magaret, 45
Caplan, G., 38
Carson, R. C., 51
Case formulation, *see* Formulation
Cashdan, S., 3, 22, 46, 136
Client (patient)
  stage relationships and, 8-11
  strategies of, 50-60

Client *(continued)*
  therapist's relation with, 1-5
  See also specific therapy technique
Client-centered therapy, 10, 36, 103
Cognitive restructuring, 2
Continuity principle, 8-9
Crisis intervention therapy, *see* Brief
    psychotherapy

Dare ploy, 73, 78
Data
  selecting, 15-16
  transforming, 17-18
Dependency strategy, 53, 54
  in group therapy, 115-116, 118
  in individual therapy, 74-76
De-roling stage
  in family therapy, 130
  in group therapy, 107, 111-115
  in sensitivity groups, 134
Direct confrontation technique, 73,
    78
Directive rules, 22-25
  See also Rules
Directive Therapy (Haley), 22-23
Dreikers, R., H. H. Mosak, and J. M.
    Schlien, 36
Dyadic bonds
  formation of, 47-50
  See also Individual therapy

Egan, G., 103, 132, 133
Ellis, A., 22
  rational-emotive therapy, 23
Emergency psychotherapy, *see* Brief
    psychotherapy
Emotional coupling, 65
  technique of, 66-67
Emotional support, PnP and, 46-47
Emotional well-being, psychotherapy
    and, 2

Encounter group, 133
Encounter-sensitivity groups, 103
Esalen Institute (Big Sur, Cal.),
    sensitivity groups and, 132
Experiences in Groups (Bion), 116

Family therapy, 103
  stages of, 129-132
Fenichel, O., 38
Ford, D. H., and H. B. Urban, 3, 5,
    24
Formulation, in psychotherapy, 13-
    18
Foulkes, S. H., and E. J. Anthony,
    103
Free-association stage, in
    psychoanalysis, 25-27
French, T. M., and F. Alexander, 5
Freud, S., 27, 38
Fromm-Reichman, F., 87

Games People Play (Berne), 42, 52
Garfield, S. L., and M. Kurz, 36
Gendlin, E., and J. Beebe, 128
Gestalt therapy, 132
Goffman, E., 43, 49
Golden, J. M., and I. N. Mensh, 36
Gouldner, A. W., 55
Greenburg, D., 53
Greenson, R., 24-25, 27, 29
Group therapy (interactional), 102-
    137
  history of, 102-103
  principles of, 103-104, 106-107
  stages of, 107-137
Group Therapy (Mullen and
    Rosenbaum), 111
Guilt, martyr strategy and, 79-80

Haley, J., 22
  directive therapy of, 22-23

Harlow, H. F., M. K. Harlow, and S. J. Suomi, 45
Heron, W., 45
Hobbs, N., 103
Homans, G., 51
Hooking stage
  in family therapy, 129-130
  in group therapy, 107-111
  in individual therapy, 62, 65-70
  in sensitivity groups, 133-34, 136
How to Be a Jewish Mother
  (Greenburg), 53
Howard, J., 118
Human Potential Movement, 132

Immediacy rule, 71
Implementation stage, of brief
  psychotherapy, 39, 40
Individual therapy (interactional),
  62-101
  adaptive strategy stage, 63, 91-97
  hooking stage, 62, 65-70
  maladaptive strategy stage, 62, 70-83
  stripping stage, 62, 83-91
  unhooking stage, 63, 97-100
Inner and Outer Space (Rabkin), 47
Insight, 1, 2
Insight Proper stage, in psychoanalysis, 25, 29-30
Intellectual validation
  interpersonal isolation and, 45
  PnP and, 45-46
Interaction Concepts of Personality
  (Carson), 51
Interactional psychotherapy
  definition of, 42-43
  dyadic bond formation and, 47-50
  foundations of, 43-47
  maladaptive strategies in, 70-83
  See also Group therapy; Individual
    therapy

Interpersonal statements, stage rules
  and, 8
Interpretive rules, 18-20

Jackson, D. D., 55, 103
Jackson, D. D., P. Watzlawick, and
  J. H. Beavin, 49-50
Jones, J. E., and J. W. Pfeiffer, 135
Jourard, S. M., 93
Joy (Schutz), 135

Kelley, H. H., and J. W. Thibaut, 51
Kiesler, D. J., 11
Klein, D., and E. Lindemann, 38
Kurz, M., and S. L. Garfield, 36

Lang, P. J., 33
Leadership, group therapy and, 113-115
Leary, T., 51
Levy, L. H., 2
Lewin, K. K., 37, 132
Lindemann, E., and D. Klein, 38
Lindesmith, A. R., and A. Strauss,
  14, 43
London, P., 7
Looping, technique of, 88

Magaret, A., and N. Cameron, 45
Maladaptive Strategies stage
  in family therapy, 130-131
  in group therapy, 115-119
  in individual therapy, 62, 70-83
  in sensitivity groups, 134, 135
Marathon groups, 137
Martyr strategy, 53-54
  in group therapy, 116-118
  in individual therapy, 79-81
Matarazzo, J. D., 36-38

McGill University, isolation
   experiments at, 45
Menninger, K., 21, 29
Mensh, I. M., and J. M. Golden, 36
Mintz, E. E., 137
Modified self-image, 2
Moreno, J. L., 102
Mosak, H. H., R. Dreikers, and J. M.
   Schlien, 36
Muench, G. A., 36
Mullen, H., and M. Rosenbaum,
   111-112, 120

National Training Laboratories
   (NTL), sensitivity groups and,
   132-133
Nemeth, C., 51
Nonexclusion principle, 10-12
Nonverbal techniques, in sensitivity
   groups, 135
Nyberg, D., 114

Ordinality principle, 9-10
Organizational change, NTL and,
   132

Pacing principle, in group therapy,
   106-107
Parental dyad, family therapy and,
   131
Patient, see Client
People need People (PnP), 43-47
Personal change, Esalen and, 132
Personality, psychotherapy and
   theory of, 5
Pfeiffer, J. W., and J. E. Jones, 135
Piaget, J., 4
Planning stage, of brief
   psychotherapy, 39
PnP, see People need People

Pragmatics of Human
   Communication (Watzlawick et
   al.), 49-50
Pratt, J. H., 102
Principles of Intensive Psycho-
   therapy (Fromm-Reichman),
   87
Procedure Frustration stage, in
   psychoanalysis, 25, 27-28
Process, definition of, 3-6
Psychoanalysis, process-stages of, 25-
   31
Psychoanalytic group therapy, 103
Psychotherapy
   definition of, 1-3
   practice of, 13-41
   training for, 7-8
   See also Stages

Rabkin, R., 47
Rational-emotive therapy (Ellis), 23
Reactive rules, 20-22
Refutation-affirmation rule, 83-84, 90
Regression (Transference Neurosis)
   stage, in psychoanalysis, 25, 28
Reinforcement, 1
Relationship stage, in brief
   psychotherapy, 39
Re-roling technique, in group
   therapy, 125
Risky revealing
   clients' practice of, 92-93
   relationship formation and, 49-50
Rogers, C., 4n., 5, 38
   client-centered therapy technique
   of, 10, 36
Rokeach, M., 59
Role behavior, 104-106
Role competency, PnP and, 44-45
Rosenbaum, M., and H. Mullen,
   111-112, 120
Ruitenbeek, H. M., 102

Rules
    directive, 22-25
    for individual therapy, 65, 71, 81-83
    interpretive, 18-20
    for group therapy, 102-137
    of systematic desensitization therapy, 34
    of psychoanalysis, 25-31
    in psychotherapy, 5, 18-25

Satir, V., 103
Schlien, J. M., H. H. Mosak, and R. Dreikers, 36
Schutz, W., 132, 135, 136
Schwartz, E. K., and A. Wolf, 103
Self-actualization, 1
Sensitivity groups, 132-137
    nonverbal techniques in, 135
Sexual strategy, 52-54
    in group therapy, 117-119
    in individual therapy, 76-79
Shepard, M., 82
Small, L., 35, 37
Small, L., and L. Bellak, 38
Social Psychology of Groups, The (Thibaut and Kelley), 51
Stage(s)
    of brief psychotherapy, 38-40
    of individual therapy, 62-99
    principles, 8-12
    of psychoanalysis, 25-31
    and psychotherapy process, 3-6
    of systematic desensitization, 34-35
    See also specific stage
Stampfl, T. G., and D. J. Levis, 137
Stoller, F. H., 137
Stone, G. P., and H. A. Farberman, 43
Strategy
    definition of, 50-51

types of, 51-56
symptoms and, 56-60
See also specific strategy
Strauss, A., and A. R. Lindesmith, 14, 43
Stripping stage
    in family therapy, 130-131
    in group therapy, 119-122
    in individual therapy, 62, 83-91
    in sensitivity groups, 134, 135
Strupp, H. H., and A. E. Bergin, 11
Sullivan H. S., "psychiatric interview," stages of, 36, 38
Suomi, S. J., Harlow, H. F., and Harlow, M. K., 45
Symbolic interactionism, 43
Symptom statements, stage rules and, 8
Symptoms, strategies and, 56-60
Systematic desensitization (Wolpe), theory of, 7, 9, 31-36

T-group (Training-group), 132-133
Technique
    of therapist, 5, 7, 18-41
    See also specific techniques
Termination (unhooking) stage
    in family therapy, 132
    in group therapy, 126-29
    in individual therapy, 63, 97-100
    in sensitivity groups, 136
Theory and Practice of Group Psychotherapy, The (Yalom), 106
Therapist
    case formulation and, 13-18
    client's relationship with, 1-5
    goal in group therapy of, 117-119
    leadership question for, 113-115
    stage, rules for, 5, 8-12
    technique of, 18-41
    See also specific therapy techniques

Therapy, *see* Interactional therapy;
    Psychotherapy
Thibaut, J. W., and H. H. Kelley, 51
Three Christs of Ypsilanti, The
    (Rokeach), 59
Training-groups (T-groups), 1322-33
Transactional feedback, technique
    of, 94-96
Transactional group therapy, 103
Transference, 1
Transference Insight stage, in
    psychoanalysis, 25, 28-30
Transference Neurosis (Regression)
    stage, in psychoanalysis, 25, 28
Transparent Self, The (Jourard), 93

Unhooking (Termination) stage
  in family therapy, 126-129
  in group therapy, 132

in individual therapy, 63, 97-100
in sensitivity groups, 136
Urban, H. B., and D. H. Ford, 3, 5,
    24

Vesting principle, in group therapy,
    106

Watson, G., 135
Watzlawick, P., J. H. Beavin, and D.
    D. Jackson, 49-50
Wolberg, L. R., 37
Wolf, A., and E. K. Schwartz, 103
Wolpe, J., systematic desensitization
    technique of, 7, 9, 31-36
Working Through stage, in
    psychoanalysis, 25, 30

Yalom, I., 12, 106, 115